SUFI SYMBOLISM

THE NURBAKHSH ENCYCLOPEDIA
OF SUFI TERMINOLOGY
(FARHANG-E NURBAKHSH)

Volume II
Love, Lover, Beloved, Allusions
and Metaphors

BY
DR. JAVAD NURBAKHSH

KHANIQAHI-NIMATULLAHI PUBLICATIONS
LONDON NEW YORK

Translated under the supervision of Dr. Javad Nurbakhsh by
Terry Graham, with the collaboration of Neil and Sima Johnston
and Ali-Reza Nurbakhsh
Designed by Jane Lewisohn.

Distributed by Routledge & Kegan Paul,
Associated Book Publishers (UK LTD)
11 New Setter Lane,
London EC4 T4EE

ISBN 0-7103-0315-7

British Library Cataloguing in Publication Data

Nurbakhsh, Javad
Sufi Symbolism: the Nurbakhsh encyclopedia of Sufi terminology *(Farhang-e Nurbakhsh)* II, love, beloved allusions and metaphors. — (The Nurbakhsh encyclopedia of Sufi terminology; 2).
1. Sufism
II. Title II. *Farhang-e Nurbakhsh.* English
III. Series
297'.4 BP189

ISBN 0-933546-31-9

Published by Khaniqahi-Nimatullahi Publications
London
41 Chepstow Place,
London W2 4TS
Great Britain
Tel: 01-229 0769

Printed by Morning Litho Printers in Great Britain.

CONTENTS

ABBREVIATIONS

For the sake of brevity, the following system of initials, indicating the titles of standard reference works on Sufi terminology, has been adopted for this *Encyclopedia.* Readers may find full bibliographical material on these texts in the Bibliography at the back of the book.

AF	*Âurâd al-aḥbâb wa foṣuṣ al-âdâb*
AM	*'Awâref al-ma'âref*
AMT	*Âthâr-e Darwish Moḥammad Ṭabasi*
AT	*Asrâr at-tauḥid*
EE	*Eṣṭelâḥât-e 'Erâqi*
ES	*Eṣṭelâḥât aṣ-ṣufiya* ('Abdo'r-Razzâq Kâshâni)
FH	*Foṣuṣ al-ḥekam*
FM	*Fotuḥât al-makkiya*
FNA	*Farhang-e Nâẓem al-aṭebbâ'* (Dehkhoda)
FRM	*Farhang-e Mo'in*
GR	*Golshan-e râz*
JA	*Rasâ'el-e jâm'-e Anṣâri*
KAM	*Kashf al-asrâr* (Maibodi)
KF	*Kashshâf eṣṭelâḥât al-fonun*
KM	*Kashf al-maḥjub*
KST	*Kholâṣa-ye sharḥ-e ta'arrof*
L	*Lawâ'eḥ-e 'Aino'l-Qoḍhât Hamadâni*
LG	*Laṭifa-ye ghaibi*
LT	*Loma' fe't-taṣawwof (Ketâb al-)*
MA	*Mashrab al-arwâḥ*
MES	*Maktubât-e Nuro'd-Din-e Esfarâyeni ba 'Alâ'd-Daula-ye Semnâni*
MH	*Meṣbâḥ al-hedâya*
MM	*Mathnawi-ye ma'nawi*
MN	*Moṣibat-nâma*
MS	*Manâzel as-sâ'erin*
NFO	*Nafaḥât al-ons*
NO	*Nur al-'olum*

RA	*Rashf al-alḥaẓ fi kâsf al-alfâẓ*
RAs	*Majmu'a-ye Rasâ'el-e Khwâja 'Abdo'llâh-e Anṣâri*
RQ	*Resâla-ye Qoshairiya*
RSh	*Rasâ'el-e Shâh Ne'mato'llâh-e Waliy*
SGR	*Sharḥ-e golshan-e râz* (Lâhiji)
SM	*Ṣad maidân*
SS	*Sharḥ-e shaṭḥiyât* (Ruzbehân)
TA	*Tadhkerat al-auliyâ'*
TJ	*Ta'rifât-e Jorjâni*
TKQ	*Tarjama-ye kalamât-e qeṣâr-e Bâbâ Ṭâher*
TS(A)	*Ṭabaqât aṣ-ṣufiya* (Anṣâri)
TS(S)	*Ṭabaqât aṣ-ṣufiya* (Solami)
TT	*Taṣawwof wạ adabiyât-e taṣawwof* (including *Mer'ât-e 'oshshâq)*

TRANSLITERATION EQUIVALENTS

Consonants

Arabic Alphabet	Latin Alphabet
ء	'
ب	b
ت	t
ث	th (s)*
ج	j
ح	ḥ
خ	kh
د	d
ذ	dh(z)
ر	r
ز	z
س	s
ش	sh
ص	ṣ
ض	ḍh (z)
ط	ṭ
ظ	ẓ
ع	'
غ	gh
ف	f
ق	q
ک	k
ل	l
م	m
ن	n
و	w(v)
ه	h
ی	y
ة	h

Long Vowels

Arabic Alphabet	Latin Alphabet
آ	â
اُو	u
اِی	i

Short Vowels

Arabic Alphabet	Latin Alphabet
اَ	a
اُ	o
اِ	e

* Letters in parantheses indicate where Persian pronounciation differs from the Arabic.

Arabic Alphabet	Latin Alphabet
Diphthongs	
اَو	au
اَى	ai

Arabic Alphabet	Latin Alphabet
Added Persian Consonants	
پ	p
چ	ch
ژ	zh
گ	g

LOVE, LOVER BELOVED
ALLUSIONS and METAPHORS

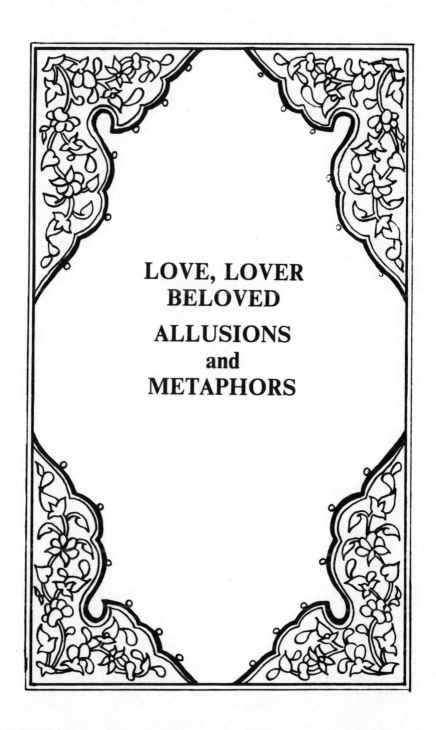

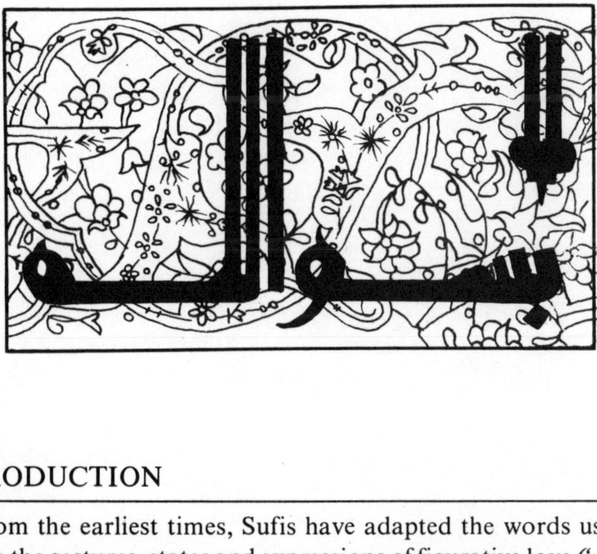

INTRODUCTION

From the earliest times, Sufis have adapted the words used to describe the gestures, states and expressions of figurative love *('eshq-e majâzi)* for the purpose of conveying the nature of True Love *('eshq-e ḥaqiqi)*. These metaphors, which gradually found their way into Sufi poetry and prose, were used not only to enhance the Sufis' message aesthetically but to enable them to express their allusions to spiritual love in a simple and appealing manner.

We have devoted this volume to an explanation of the technical terms used by the Sufis to describe love, the lover, and the Beloved.

SEEKING *(ṭalab)*

In Sufi terminology, 'seeking' connotes the pain and attraction which cause the novice wayfarer to set out in quest of the Divine Reality *(ḥaqiqat).* As such, it is a feature of the early stages of the Sufi path *(sair-o soluk).*[1]

In his *Manṭeq aṭ-ṭair (The Conference of the Birds),* 'Aṭṭâr designates 'seeking' as the 'first valley' to be crossed in the traversal of the Sufi path.

> I'll not give up seeking until I gain fulfillment,
> Till the soul reaches the Beloved or simply leaves the body.
>
> Ḥâfeẓ

'Seeking' is said to represent the search for God, irrespective of whether one is [consciously] attracted or not. This 'search' usually involves a relationship between the devotee and the object of devotion. (In any case, 'seeking' is motivated by innate predisposition, regardless of the 'seeker's' aim.)[2]

EE 54

'Seeking' is said to symbolise the search for God through servanthood *('obudiyat).*

1. *Sair* denotes inward, spiritual motion, and *soluk* denotes the observance of outward conduct.
2. Cf. Sharafo'd-din Olfati Tabrizi, *Rashf al-alḥâẓ fi kashf al-alfâz.* ed. Mâyel Herawi, (Tehran, 1983), p.41.

This seeking is the key to all that you desire;
It represents your battle colours and your troops in
victory.

Keep striving ever onward to increase this seeking,
Until your heart is freed from the prison of this body.[1]

TT 213

In the terminology of the wayfarers, 'seeking' is said to signify the spending of night and day in God's remembrance, whether in solitude or in society, at home or at work. When offered the world and its blessings, or the hereafter and its paradise, the seeker rejects them both, accepting, rather, the afflictions *(balâ')* and tribulations *(meḥnat)* of the world. While everyone else is busy repenting from sin, from fear of falling into hell, the seeker 'repents' from lawful things in order to avoid stumbling into heaven. While others pursue their personal ends, the seeker searches for God, to view God, taking his every step with trust *(tawakkol)* in God. He regards the asking for things from others as polytheism *(sherk),* and the asking of things from God as a mark of shame. Affliction and tribulation, bestowal or witholding, acceptance or rejection, are all the same to him.

KF 900

The 'seeking' of a thing begins when one comes to know a part of that thing. Whoever does not 'seek' well and is not serious in his 'seeking' will not attain what he seeks, for finding what one seeks is the result of sincere 'seeking'.

BT 533

In his *One Hundred Fields* Ansâri describes the forty-fourth field as that of 'seeking', which arises from the field of hope. The Koran speaks of those who "...seek the manner of approaching their Lord, which of them will be nearest." (Koran XVII: 57).

'Seeking' involves searching and striving and consists of three parts: 'seeking' of freedom, of merit, and of God.

The 'seeking of freedom' is born of the pain of severance from God, of shame from God's reproach, and of the humiliation of being veiled from God. This is the 'seeking of the destitute'.

1. MM III 1443; V 1735.

The 'seeking of merit' is the seeking of heaven, intercession, and happiness. This is the seeking of the warrior.

The 'seeking of God' is a formidable commitment, involving renunciation of this world and the next. People view this lightly, failing to take it seriously. People normally find a thing after seeking it, but the seekers of God seek Him after finding Him. They are the ones who are dear to Him.

SM 42

The reality of 'seeking' is present in every heart. The one who searches consciously is a great man, for the pain of seeking is great. It requires a man who can take this pain and he must have insight. If you would be a seeker, purify your way; turn your back on the material world. Although the wilderness must be traversed, it is erroneous to take your self as a travelling companion. One who is fit for such an undertaking must be a 'man' indeed; he must be detached and must have pain for God alone.

In seeking the Traceless One *(bi-athar)*, even the most devoted lose heart, for no one knows the secret of how to go about it.

My friend, if it exists, why go looking for it, and if it does not, why try to find it? There is no separate existence before Oneness *(aḥadiyat)*. The existence of things is nothing; reflect upon your own condition, and recall those who have passed away before you, for the farthest degree of every worshipper's devotional practice consists in this.

RJ 114

Whenever the gnostic, in the course of 'seeking' God, becomes annihilated in God by God, he finds Him. He seeks his own 'being' in the contemplative vision *(moshâhada)* of God, so that he may derive pleasure *(ledhdhat)* from the benefits of God's Majesty *(jalâl)*. This 'seeking' represents a descent from the station of subsistence to that of annihilation, because in the reality of Divine Unity *(tauḥid)* the gnostic is astounded and bedazzled. God said: "They seek God's bounty and acceptance" (XLVIII: 29).

Ḥallâj said, "The gnostic's seeking is due to his absence from himself in God. When he attains the reality of gnosis, the station of 'seeking' falls away from him, and seeking becomes activated in his essence without him being aware of it."

MA 40

It takes a man who, at every moment, in seeking and waiting,
Is able to cast off his soul a hundred times on the Way.
Not a moment has he respite from seeking;
Not an instant can he find repose.
If he should ever pause from his seeking,
He'd be a graceless apostate to this Way.

SGR 261

Abo'l-'Abbâs Qaṣṣâb said, "If anyone other than God were to seek God, then God would be twofold; it is God who seeks God, God who finds God, God who knows God.

TS(A) 643

There is pleasure in 'seeking', but no pleasure in 'finding'. 'Finding' involves a blow which shatters you completely.

TS(A) 149

Bâyazid gives the following account of his own experience of 'seeking': "When I was a novice I made four mistakes: I supposed that I was remembering God, that I knew God, that I loved God, and that I was seeking God. When I reached the end of the Way, I saw that God's remembrance of me had preceded mine of him, that his knowledge of me had preceded mine of him, that his love had preceded mine, and that he had sought me first, before I could seek him."

TS(S) 64

DEVOTION *(erâdat)*

In Sufi terminology, the word *erâdat*[1] signifies the Sufi's complete attention to God. It is also said to refer to the special attention of the disciple to the Master of the Path.

'Devotion' is a ray of the light from the divine quality of 'willing', as in God's name: 'The Willer' *(morid).*

1. From the Arabic root *r-u-d* meaning 'to desire', are derived the words, *erâdat, morid.* and *morâd.* The *morid* is the 'one who is devoted' 'the desirer', and *morâd,* the 'object of desire or devotion'.

One can only become a 'disciple' *(morid)* when God has revealed this attribute in a theophany, such that the light of 'devotion' is projected in the devotee's heart. For this reason, 'devotion' is the precondition for setting out on the way towards God.

'True devotion' *(erâdat-e ḥaqiqi)* is where the disciple is perfectly obedient to the master *(morâd)*, complying with his every command and desiring nothing other than what the master desires. In contrast, 'false devotion' *(erâdat-e ghalaṭ)* is where the disciple does not follow the real master but, instead, makes a master out of his own selfish desires.

TKQ 523

The existence of man and angel
is based on love;
Practice devotion so that
you may attain bliss.

Ḥâfeẓ

I place my head devotedly
upon the threshold of the friend,
So that whatever happens to me
is what the friend desires.

Ḥâfeẓ

Concerning the 'devotion of the wayfarers', Ruzbehân writes:

Once the heart is set alight by the flame shot from the bow of theophany into the inner consciousness of the inner consciousness *(serr-e serr)*, 'devotion' appears, activating the innate aptitude of the spirit, which is the steed of the armies of gnosis in the valley of nearness *(qorb)*, travelling towards the source of pre-eternity *(azal)*. God says: "Indeed, He who has given the Koran for a law, will surely bring you back home again".[1]

Ḥallâj said, " 'Devotion' is the need for wisdom and the activation of the heart."

MA 31

1. Koran XXVIII: 85.

Concerning the 'devotion of the sincere' *(ṣeddiqân)*, Ruzbehân writes:

One who awakes from the sleep of oblivion begins to burn and admonitions from Reality cause reprehensible behaviour to fall away from him. At this time, he sees his *nafs*[1] flee from servanthood and his heart become veiled from awareness of Lordship *(robubiyat)*. He turns towards the realm of Command *(amr)* and seeks the straight path by the light of his intellect and faith, from whomever possesses any awareness of God. He then becomes excited, experiences the onrush of infusions *(wâred)* from the unseen, and wants, with all his heart, to witness God; at this point he becomes the disciple of a master. He then becomes attached to that master, is slain with the sword of the master's loving-kindness, and surrenders to God's wrath and grace, and whatever his *nafs* and desires command is burnt by the breath of the master. When God sees the sincere one in this state, He, through the spiritual realities of the Unseen *(ma'âni-ye ghaib)*, helps him to accept the subtleties of those realities and become receptive to the subtlest of those subtleties, so that he behaves in a manner consistent with them.

Thereupon, the disciple attains the reality of 'devotion', desiring nothing from God other than what God wants of him. The foregoing describes the reality of the disciple's devotion, the way of the wayfarers and the path of the rightly guided. The key factor in all of this is love's attraction *(jazba-ye 'eshq)*, and exposure to the fire of yearning *(shauq)* on the part of a nature predisposed to gnosis.

It has been said that 'devotion' involves the stimulation of understanding and of pain in the heart. The Koran says, "It is he whose breast God opens up for the surrender [to Him], so that he follows a light from his Lord." (XXXIX: 22).

Ḥallâj said, " 'Devotion' is the sudden falling of the Lord's loving kindness into the heart."

MA 52

From Ebn 'Arabi's standpoint 'devotion' means the exclusive attention one has to the acquisition of gnosis of God, through which one may gain knowledge of God by way of revelation, not through intellectual and logical reasoning.

FM II 521

1. Unless otherwise specified, the Arabic word *nafs* as used in this book connotes 'ego', 'self', 'carnal soul' and the desires that stem therefrom.

'Devotion' is a flaming brand from the fire of loving-kindness which enkindles response to the appeals of Reality.

ES 27

INCLINATION *(mail)*

'Inclination' is said to be the tendency to return to one's origin without consciousness of the origin or goal, just as the natural tendency of minerals is to revert involuntarily to their constituent elements and of those elements, in turn, to involuntarily return to their origin.

EE 53

Until post-eternity the habitants of both the worlds
Have an inclination towards you, whether knowing you or
not.

'Aṭṭâr

DESIRE *(ârzu)*

'Desire' is the inclination towards one's origin, accompanied by a small share of awareness and knowledge about that origin and goal.

EE 54

O Beloved, out of desire for you
My soul has burned away.

My pain has gone beyond all bounds
In fervent melancholy for your face.

'Aṭṭâr

WISH *(tamannâ)*

'Wish' is said to represent the seeking of something, whether it be possible or not.

TJ 92

When Rowaim was asked if the disciple should 'wish', he said,

"He should not wish; rather, he should hope, because to wish is to view things through the *nafs,* whereas to hope is to envision spiritual advancement. Wishing is an attribute of the *nafs,* while hope is an attribute of the heart."

LT 227

Abu Sa'id Kharrâz said, "Whoever thinks that one may achieve something without suffering is wishful, while one who believes that one must suffer to achieve, makes trouble for himself."

TS(A) 181

Whenever yearning *(shauq)* attains its limit of perfection, the least that the lover *(moshtâq)* wishes for is the detachment of his spirit from his material form and its attainment of the beauty of God. His highest 'wish' is for visionary revelation without veiling and viewing without torment, that is, the torment of separation [from God]. According to the Koran: "So, long for death if you are truthful"(II: 94).

The gnostic said, " 'Wishing' is the experience of the fresh sweetness of a station, the fragrant breaths of which are scented by the one who longs for God in a state of loss of self."

MA 108

I am needful but cannot beg;
　　what need is there
To express a wish before the one
　　who is magnanimous?

Ḥâfeẓ

LOVE, KINDNESS *(mehr)*

'Mehr'[1] is inclination towards, and return to one's origin. It is associated with awakened perception *(edrâk)*, its preconditions are 'seeking' *(ṭalab)* and 'yearning' *(shauq)*.

1. The Persian term *mehr* is less emphatic than but synonomous with the Arabic term *mahabba* according to the Anandrâj and Vullers dictionaries.

What I have and you do not
is such love and fidelity;
What you have and I do not
is such patience and tranquillity.

TT 229-230

'Mehr' represents loving-kindness *(maḥabbat)* towards one's origin with knowledge and awareness gained by perception of the goal.

KF 1346

'Mehr' is said to represent 'friendship' *(dusti)* for God, accompanied by 'seeking' and 'striving'.

EE 54

What is kindness? To make a breast out of stone
And make both worlds your suckling babes.

MN 42

MELANCHOLY *(saudâ')*

Conventionally, this word connotes 'intense inclination' *(mail)* or, simply, 'love' *('eshq)*.

'Melancholy' is said to be the effect of Divine attraction, which results in complete absorption in God and detachment from self.

When melancholy has descended
into the core of someone's heart,
It follows that his heart and soul
must one day, by means of it, depart.

TT 207

O you who deny the world of the Sufis,
What do you know of their melancholy
and their preoccupation?

Sa'di

One who has not gone mad from this melancholy,
O 'Erâqi, tell him he has no sense.

'Erâqi

The pain of melancholy for you
is not confined to me alone.
There are many of us
who have been burned up by this fire.

Kamâl Khojandi

My head is full of melancholy for you
and my soul in an uproar over you;
A world writhes in agony, burning
with the fire of melancholy for you.

'Aṭṭâr

LOVE, FRIENDSHIP *(dusti)*

'Friendship' is said to be Divine loving-kindness *(maḥabbat)* in the pre-eternity of pre-eternities *(azal-e âzâl)* (which preceeds mankind's love for God).

The Koran says, "He loves them and they love Him[1],"
Which shows that God initiated the covenant of
loving-kindness.[2]

TT 197

It is the fortunate one who has a friend like you
To protect him from his foes in both worlds.

'Erâqi

'Aṭṭâr's heart discovered the secret of friendship
Only when he discovered that he was his own foe.

'Aṭṭâr

1. Koran V: 54.
2. Cf. KF 1557.

The proof that one has attained 'friendship' is that the two worlds are flung into the sea. The sign that 'friendship' has been realised is that one is concerned with nothing but God. 'Friendship' is initially warmth, and finally illumination. In the beginning, 'friendship' is helplessness; in the middle, expectation; and in the end, 'beholding' *(didâr).*

KAM VII 513

'Friendship' is said to be between two, while three makes a crowd. But in this 'friendship' all is You, and 'I' makes a crowd.

KAM VII 310

The sign that 'friendship' has been established is 'contentment' *(reḍhâ').* The value of 'friendship' increases through 'fidelity' *(wafâ').* The whole of the substance of the treasure of 'friendship' is light. The fruit of the tree of 'friendship' is all 'joy' *(sorur).* Whoever remains apart from the two worlds, in 'friendship' with God, is justified in doing so. Whoever seeks reward for 'friendship' from the Friend is ungrateful. 'Friendship' means 'friendship with God'; friendship with anything else is merely temptation.

KAM III 155

'Friendship' has three stages: 'passion' *(hawâ)* which is an attribute of the body, 'loving-kindness' *(maḥabbat)* which is an attribute of the heart; and 'love' *('eshq)* an attribute of the soul. Passion is based on the *nafs,* loving-kindness on the heart, and love on the soul. That love which is an attribute of the soul has, in turn, three aspects, the first being 'truthfulness' *(râsti)*; the second, 'drunkenness' *(masti)*; and the last, 'nothingness' *(nisti).*

KAM II 44

Do you know why the tale of 'friendship' is so long? Because the Friend has no need. If you accept one of His friends, you gain deliverance; and if one of His friends accepts you, you become linked to Him.

RAs 21

Abo'l-Ḥasan Kharaqâni said, "The food and wine of the *javânmardân*[1] is friendship with God.

TA 700

Abu Sa'id Abe'l-Khair recounted how Shebli once told of two friends who were inseparable. It happened once that they had to embark on a ship to cross a sea. When the ship reached the middle of the sea, one of them, leaning over the side, fell into the water. His friend jumped in after him. The anchor was lowered and divers leapt in to rescue them, bringing them both aboard safe and sound. After a little while they recovered, and the one who had first fallen in said to his companion, "I fell into the water by accident. What brought you in?" His friend replied, "I was absent from myself in you; so I considered myself to be you."

AT 259

'Awareness' is the state of hirelings *(mozdurân)*; 'acquaintanceship', the quality of those who are 'guests'; and 'friendship' the sign of those who are intimate and close. 'Hirelings' are paid. 'Guests' are entertained, and the intimate are privy to secrets. The 'hireling' is paid what he is worth; the 'guest' merits the hospitality of the host; and the one who is intimate is steeped in the vision of God.

KAM I 787

Ansâri gives sixteen qualities as preconditions for friendship:

Unlimited generosity, unblemished integrity, co-operation without expectation, association without criticism, soundness of speech, service without resentment, love without misgivings, discretion in seeing, acquaintanceship without prejudice, absolute silence, straightforwardness, control of *nafs*, eating with appreciation, assumption of responsibility for the offence of a friend, prayer by night and pilgrimage by day, pure-hearted aspiration *(hemmat),* and guidance from a master, in order that one's efforts may reap fulfilment on the Day of Resurrection.

RAs 139

1. *Javânmard* signifies someone who dedicates his being and everything he possesses to his friend, or, indeed, to anyone, expecting nothing in return.

'Loving-kindness' is 'friendship' with God which is preceded by God's friendship, as referred to in the Koranic verse, "He loves them and they love Him" (V:53), where "He loves them" preceeds "...they love Him."

The trace of familiarity existed
before the trace of the two worlds;
Loving-kindness was designed,
not now, but in pre-eternity.

Ḥâfeẓ

'Loving-kindness' is said to be friendship with God, which is without cause, self-interest, or outward expression.

EE 54

'Loving-kindness' is 'Divine friendship' *(welâyat)* which descends from the Beloved *(ma'shuq)* to the lover *('âsheq)*, whether he chooses it or not.

AMT 376

'Loving-kindness' is said to signify the realization of a state of completely concentrated attention on absolute beauty itself, on the level of the transconscious *(khafi)*[1] which causes the fetters of temporal being to be sundered.

TT 227

Tahanawi ellucidates eleven stages of *mahabbat*, the first being 'concordance' *(mowâfeqat)* where one regards the enemies of God, namely the world, Satan and the *nafs* as one's own foes, while loving the friends of God at the same time, displaying 'loving-kindness' towards them, and cherishing their commands in the hope of winning a place in their hearts.

The second stage is 'inclination' *(mail)*.

The third stage is 'mutual intimacy' *(mo'ânesat)*. This means

1. There are seven levels of heart consciousness, 1) physical nature *(tab')*, 2) the *nafs*, 3) the heart *(qalb)*, 4) the spirit *(ruḥ)*, 5) the inner consciousness *(serr)*, 6) the transconscious *(khafi)* and 7) the supraconscious *(akhfâ')*.

fleeing from all in seeking God at every 'moment' *(waqt)*. "The one who becomes intimate with God dreads what is other than God."

The fourth stage is 'affection' *(mawaddat)*, which means absorbing oneself in the seclusion of the heart in abjectness, and 'weeping' at the height of 'longing' *(eshtiyâq)* and distress.

The fifth stage, 'passion' *(hawâ)*, is the heart's constant striving to the point of melting.

The sixth stage is 'familiarity' *(khollat)*, which means filling one's whole body with the Friend and emptying it of what is 'other'.

The seventh stage is 'loving-kindness' *(maḥabbat)*, which means purifying oneself of undesirable traits, so that one may become characterised by praiseworthy ones. The more the *nafs* is purged of what is undesirable, the closer the spirit moves to 'loving-kindness'.

The eighth stage, 'enamourment' *(shaghaf)*, means being so inflamed with 'yearning' *(shauq)* that one tears the veil from the heart, yet holds back tears from the eyes, so that others remain unaware of this 'loving-kindness', for 'loving-kindness' is the mystery of Lordship *(robubiyat)* and disclosure of this is 'unbelief' *(kofr)*, unless one is overcome by a state.

The ninth stage, 'enthralment' *(ṭa'im)* means making oneself the slave of 'loving-kindness' and becoming characterised by detachment from the world *(tajrid)* and detachment from self *(tafrid)*.

The tenth stage, 'enravishment' *(walah)*, means holding the mirror of the heart before the Beauty of the Friend, becoming drunk with the wine of that Beauty, and going the way of the love-sick.

The eleventh and final stage is 'love' *('eshq)*, which means being in distress and losing oneself.[1]

KF 270

'Loving-kindness' is concordance with the Beloved *(maḥbub)* in whatever He likes or dislikes.

AF 53

Ma'ruf Karkhi said, "Loving-kindness is not taught in a wordly way, but comes from God's generosity and grace."

TA 328

1. For a further discussion of the stages of love, see Massignon, L. *The Passion of Hallaj* Vol. I p. 340. Bollingen Series XCVIII, Princeton, 1982.

Asked how one might detect 'loving-kindness' Yaḥyâ ebn Mo'âdh said, "By the fact that it is neither increased by favour nor diminished by ill favour."

TA 372

Abu 'Othmân Ḥiri said, "The quality of 'loving-kindness' is called such because it obliterates everything in the heart save the Beloved."

TA 481

'Loving-kindness' is the 'inclination' of the 'beautiful' *(jamil)* for 'beauty' *(jamâl)*, inspired by 'contemplative vision' *(moshâhada)*. 'Ordinary loving-kindness' is the heart's inclination to contemplate the beauty of the Attributes. 'Special loving-kindness' is the spirit's inclination towards witnessing the Essence, the sunlight rising from the horizon of the Essence.

RSh II 175

In the early stages, 'loving-kindness' is gratification through worship, along with indifference towards losing what is other than God. In the final stages, it is the 'friendship' of the Essence with itself in one-ness *(aḥadiyat)* through the annihilation of any trace of the transitory in the essence of pre-eternity.

RSh IV 78

The domain of 'loving-kindness' includes neither ritual nor worship, nor does protocol or ceremony have any place in this domain; and those who place importance on form have no awareness of what these words mean. The way-stations of this domain differ greatly from one another. 'Loving-kindness' is included in the revealed Law *(shari'at)*. It cannot be communicated outwardly. This is a wine which must be drunk, not taken on hearsay. You must attain this station, not just inquire about it.

'Loving-kindness' is of three kinds: causal *('ellati)*, created, and true *(ḥaqiqi)*.

'Causal loving-kindness' is 'passion' *(hawâ)*; 'created loving-kindness' is ordainment *(qaḍhâ')*; and 'true loving-kindness' is bestowal *('aṭâ')*. That 'loving-kindness' which springs from cause descends upon the *nafs*, causing its degeneration. The 'created loving-kindness' descends upon the heart, obliterating it. The loving-kindness which arises from Reality *(ḥaqiqat)* establishes itself in the soul, annihilating the soul as something 'other' than Reality, and subsequently brings it into existence in Reality.

RAs 112

FUNDAMENTAL LOVING-KINDNESS
(maḥabbat-e aṣliya)

'Fundamental loving-kindness' is the loving-kindness which exists inherently between the Essence and itself. It is the foundation of all the varieties of loving-kindness. Furthermore, whatever loving-kindness exists between two individuals is due to similarities in their essences, attributes, ranks, states or activities.

ES 338

LOVING-KINDNESS COMPARED WITH MODESTY
(moqâyesa-ye maḥabbat wa ḥayâ)

Bondâr ebn Ḥosain said, "Loving-kindness is desiring, which involves suffering, while modesty is self-consciousness. The one who has loving-kindness is a seeker who is 'absent' from himself, while the modest one is 'present' to himself. The difference is that loving-kindness thrives where there is absence from self, while modesty arises only before that which is visible. The absent one, a stranger to himself, is not like the present one who is close to himself.

TS(S) 492

THE RELATIONSHIP BETWEEN LOVING-KINDNESS AND DEVOTION *(râbeta-ye maḥabbat bâ erâdat)*

'Loving-kindness' connotes 'confirmed devotion'. One might say, either, "I am devoted to this task," or "I have loving-kindness in relation to, or towards this task." The difference between 'loving-kindness' and 'devotion' is that 'devotion' is for the attributes or acts of the Beloved, as when one says, "I am devoted to your magnanimity." This is devotion to an attribute. If it is devotion to the essence of the Beloved, in most cases it is 'loving-kindness'.

EK 338

LOVE, FAMILIARITY *(khollat)*

'Familiarity' signifies the devotee's realisation *(taḥaqqoq)* of an Attribute of God, such that God possesses him, penetrating his entire being, and not a particle of his being remains empty of God's theophany. In this state, the devotee becomes the mirror of God.

ES 161

Open your eye and sit at the table of God's
Intimate Friend;[1]
Seek profit from the mystery of love,
not from lentils and bread.

Maghrebi

LOVE, CHARITY *(ḥobb)*[2]

'Love' is a particular kind of attachment related to 'devotion'. It is a motivating force that draws the lover *(moḥebb)* towards the Beloved *(maḥbub)*.

'Love' is the passion *(hawâ)* which frees itself of other attachments by attaching itself to the Way of God. Hence, whenever passion becomes liberated from and purged of the turbidity associated with other attachments, it is called 'love'.

FM II 335

The sign of 'love' is the purification of the lover's heart from the turbidity which comes from external attractions and internal desires. Therefore, the lover must seek only the Beloved from the Beloved and follow no path but that of the Beloved.

RSh I 208

1. Referring to the Prophet Abraham, whose Islamic sobriquet is *Khalilo'llah,* the 'friend of God'.
2. The Arabic word *ḥobb* is a verbal noun which is used throughout the Koran to signify love. Other key terms which are nouns and participles derived from the same root, (ḥ-b-b) and which appear later in the text, are listed below:
moḥebb: love (active participle).
maḥbub: Beloved (passive participle),
ḥabib: lover or beloved, depending on context (noun of agent),
maḥabba: love (abstract verbal noun).

'Love' may be engendered by either beauty or 'beneficence' *(eḥsân)*. If it is the former, it is a case of "Indeed, God, the Beautiful, loves beauty,[1] and if the latter, it is a case of "Beneficence is perfected through God and there is no beneficent one but God."

RSh I 211

This blindness of mine is the blindness of love.
Loving a thing makes one blind and deaf.

MM III 2362

I said that I risked blame
 if I joined the circle of the Friend;
By God, we've never heard of love without blame therein.

Ḥâfeẓ

What is love? Not to be concerned with your soul
To be close to the Beloved and to cast your soul away.

MN 42

KINDS OF LOVE, CHARITY *(aqsâm-e ḥobb)*

Divine love: God's love for us, and sometimes our 'love' for Him.

Spiritual love: one's striving to please the Beloved *(maḥbub),*desiring nothing of the Beloved in return, but rather, placing oneself wholeheartedly at the Beloved's disposal.

Natural love: that in which one is concerned with satisfying one's personal desires without consideration of the wishes of the Beloved.

FM II 327

1. *Traditions of the Prophet,* Vol I (New York: 1981) p. 55-56.

Constancy in 'love' *(ḥobb, 'eshq)* or 'passsion' *(hawâ)* is known as *wodd.* Whenever one arrives at any degree of constancy and permanence in the possesion of any of these qualities, it is known as 'amity'. According to the Koran: "...the Beneficent will appoint for them love," (XIX: 96). That is to say, constancy in 'loving-kindness' before God.

FM II 337

In Sufi terminology, *wodd* is the 'love' which stimulates the lover *(moḥebb)* to become annihilated from his *nafs.*

KF 1470

The prophets were the people of love,
Their oneness came to be understood as such.

MM VI 2447

Due to the benefit that the lover receives from 'loving-kindness', his loving becomes purified and he becomes close to the ordeal of 'love'. Because of his pure servanthood he passes this ordeal and arrives at the station of intimacy, the veins of gnosis exuding in his heart. At this point he reaches the station of 'amity' from that of 'love' *(ḥobb).* He maintains stability *(tamkin)*[1] in the face of whatever decrees may flow to him from Lordship *(robubiyat)*, not becoming veiled by the tests of those decrees. At this time, the cord of pre-eternal selection joins with the cord of post-eternal favour, and the one who enjoys 'amity' recognises through God his own station of 'amity' in the 'amity' of pre-eternity. His aspiration is drawn to the station of certitude *(yaqin)* in which he is secure, and his phial of mysteries and his vessels of truth remain unshattered by the stones of wrath. Thereafter, he lives on enjoying the Attributes, through which he becomes hidden in the Essence Itself, whereby he attains the ultimate of 'love', of which 'amity' is the reality.

The gnostic said, "Amity signifies Union *(weṣâl)* without change of states."

MA 96

1. For a full discussion of *tankin* see: The authors, *Sufism III* p.113.

THE DIFFERENCE BETWEEN 'LOVE, CHARITY' AND 'LOVE, AMITY' *(farq bain-e ḥobb wa wood)*

'Distance' *(bo'd)* and 'nearness' *(qorb)* obtain in *ḥobb,* whereas in *wodd* neither they nor separation of any kind exist. The one who enjoys *ḥobb* is at the stage of the 'truth of certitude' *(ḥaqqo'l-yaqin),* while the one who experiences *wodd* is at the stage of the 'eye of certitude' *('aino'l-yaqin).* The one who is concerned with safeguarding himself is at the stage of the 'knowledge of certitude' *('elmo'l-yaqin).* Furthermore, *wodd* involves Union *(weṣâl)* and not 'interrupted union' *(mowâṣela)* because Union is stable, and 'interrupted union' is subject to change in states.

LT 229

ARDENT LOVE *(mawaddat)*

In the terminology of the wayfarers, 'ardent love' is one of the levels of 'loving-kindness', being the 'excitement' *(hayajân)* of the heart, characterised by 'passion'. It has five degrees: the first is lamentation and anxiety, and anxiety which, at this station, is all mourning, moaning and crying out and restlessness; the second is weeping; the third is 'grief' *(ḥasrat),* in which station the wretched one in 'ardent love' grieves for his cherished moments which have been wasted and regrets every instant which has passed without his Beloved; the fourth is 'reflection' *(tafakkor)* on the Beloved, as the Koran says: "Indeed, therein are signs for those who reflect" (XIII: 3), and as in the Prophetic Tradition: "The reflection of an hour is better than sixty years' devotion, for reflection on the Causer *(maujeb)* brings nearness to Him[1]; the final degree is 'contemplation' *(morâqaba)* of the Beloved, being the finest and most intense of stations. O dear one, you have heard how once, when 'Ali, the Commander of the Faithful, was saying his prayers, his face went pale, his heart seized up, and he fell unconscious. When he was asked what the matter was, he explained, "While I was contemplating God in my prayers, I was struck with shame at my transgressions."

KF 1470

1. The number of years differ in different versions of this Tradition. Cf. the author's *Traditions of the Prophet* Vol. 2 (New York: 1983) p.l: and Hojwiri, *Kashf al-maḥjub* (Leningrad: 1926) p. 135.

When ardent love is steadfast in service,
What better work is there for you than this?

Nâṣer Khosrau

PASSION *(hawâ)*

'Passion' causes the effacement of the 'will' of the lover in that of the Beloved. It is the first feeling for the Beloved which passes through the heart.

Whoever experiences passion thus
Possesses our desire within his heart.

'Passion' can be defined as two aspects of 'love' *(ḥobb).*

The first aspect is that which involves the apparition of 'love' from the 'unseen world' *('âlam-e ghaib)* in the heart of the lover, which may be caused by the audition, vision or beneficence of the Beloved. Of these causes the most complete and important is vision, which undergoes no alteration in the course of a direct encounter with the Beloved. 'Love' caused by hearing of the Beloved may be changed by direct encounter with Him. When the lover experiences 'love' by observing his Beloved's beneficence, it is merely causal, disappearing when its cause is forgotten.

The second aspect is the passion or desire which one has for friends. Everyone is enjoined to abandon their own interests, as God commanded David, saying, "Do not follow desire" (XXXVIII: 25), by which He meant, 'Do not follow the things that you love, but, rather, follow what I love, and that is what I prescribe for you.'

Give up pining for the world if you pine for me;
Give up your own passion if you have desire for me.

RSh I 211-14

I have a desire hidden in my breast;
If I lose my head, it will be from that passion.

Ḥâfeẓ

PERDITION-IN-LOVE *(gharâm)*

'Perdition-in-love' is said to represent obliteration in the Beloved.

God said: "Indeed, the torment thereof is perdition," (XXXV: 65), referring to those who are obliterated, where 'vision' *(shohud)* of the Beloved causes the obliteration of the lover. 'Perdition-in-love' is the most perfect of the attributes of 'love' and has the profoundest influence of all the attributes of 'love'.

RSh I 214

ENRAVISHMENT *(walah)*

'Enravishment' is said to mean 'being distraught' in love *('eshq)* and being excessive in ecstasy and love.

Since through enravishment you have become
'One who is God's', God will be yours![1]

MM 1939

'Enravishment' is one of the stations of the lovers *('âsheq)*. 'Enravishment' in love signifies the absence of the lover in the Beloved *(ma'shuq)*, when the lover is enravished and adrift between union and separation. Whenever the conventions of intellect and knowledge fall away from the lover and he is unable to find a way out for his enravished spirit confied by the contraction which comes from the realm of ordainment *(jabarut)*, he becomes 'enravished' by God in God. This is a beautiful quality in the state of love.

I have heard it said that Dho'n-Nun used to pray "O light of the eyes of the gnostics. O Beloved *(ḥabib)* of enravished hearts."

The gnostic stated, "enravishment" is the heart's infatuation *(hayamân)* with the Beauty *(jamâl)* of the Lord."

MA 123

LOVE, EROS *('eshq)*[2]

'Love' is the extreme expression of 'loving-kindness'. It is a fire which descends upon the heart of the lover of God, consuming all but

1. Refering to the Prophetic Tradition "He who gives himself up entirely to God is united with Him." See Foruzanfar *Aḥâdith-e Mathnawi* (Tehran: 1982) No. 43.
2. See the author's *In the Tavern of Ruin* (New York: 1979) p. 22-32.

God. This 'love' is Divine. It befalls one, it cannot be learned.

'Love' is said to signify 'friendship *(dusti)* with God', based on seeking and total effort.

RA 41

The term, 'love', usually refers to the inner consciousness, and the essence of the intellect.

The spirit has two aspects:

The first is its concentration on the realm of Unity *(waḥdat)* and the domain of the Sacred. In this context the spirit is called 'love'. Sometimes 'love' denotes the essence of the spirit's attention and attraction towards divine unity.

The second is the spirit's attention towards the realm of multiplicity, involving the expansion of knowledge of multiplicity. This aspect, in turn, has two types. The first is the perception of universal truths and sacred spiritual realities. This type is known as the 'other-worldly intellect' *('aql-e ma'âd)*. The second is the perception of the state's particulars, the activities of the senses, and material objects. This type is called the 'worldly-intellect' *('aql-e ma'âsh)* or the 'partial intellect'. This latter form of intellect is the opposite of 'love'.

Once love has come to dwell in a breast,
It makes the soul despair of existence.
Love of the Beloved is fire; the intellect smoke.
When love arrives, intellect flees.

TT 215-216

When Abu Sa'id Abe'l-Khair was asked about 'love', he said, "Love is God's trap."

AT 324

It is recounted that [on the day he was to be executed] Ḥallâj was asked by a darvish the meaning of 'love'. He said, "You will see today, and tomorrow, and the day after." That day he was killed; on the following day his body was burned; and the day after, his ashes were thrown to the winds. This is the meaning of 'love'.

TA 591

Abo'l-Ḥasan Kharaqâni said, "A particle of love appeared from the realm of the Unseen *('alam-e ghaib)*, scented the breasts of all the lovers,[1] found no receptive heart and so returned to the Unseen."

TA 697

He stated further, "Love is a blessing from that sea which creatures cannot traverse. It is a fire through which the soul cannot pass. It comes and goes without the devotee's knowing. Whatever one commits to this sea, there are only two things that one receives from it: anguish *(anduh)* and need *(niyâz)*."

TA 708

'Love' devours people and without love people are base. Love has neither name nor shame, and enjoys neither war nor peace.

RJ 21

If you are bound by 'love', do not seek release. If you are slain by love, do not seek retribution. Love is a consuming fire and a boundless sea. It is both soul and Beloved of souls. It is the story without end and the pain without a cure. The intellect is confounded in perceiving it, and the heart is incapable of receiving it, while the lover is its sacrificial victim. It is the concealer of the manifest and the revealer of the hidden.

'Love' is the life of the heart. If it is motionless, it pulls the heart apart, extracting all that is other than itself. If it comes storming in, it turns the heart inside out, disgracing the heart before all. Love is not pain, but it brings forth pain. It is not affliction, but it visits affliction on one's head. Just as it is the quickener of life, so it is the bringer of death. However much it is the potion of ease, it is just as much the cause of disease. 'Loving-kindness' consumes the lover[2] and leaves the Beloved,[3] while love consumes the 'seeker' and leaves the Sought.

RJ 125

1. *Moḥebbân.*
2. *Moḥebb.*
3. *Maḥbub.*

Since there can be no excess or extreme in the eternal attributes, and 'love', if arrived at, is the extreme expression of 'loving-kindness', the term 'love' and 'lover' cannot be used in reference to God.

RSh I 210

In the creed of the lovers, the situation is different,
And from this rare wine there's a different languor.
Whatever science you've learned in school
Is another matter from that of love.

Rumi

The one who is brought to life by love
 will never die;
Our perpetuity is recorded
 in the annals of the world.

Ḥâfeẓ

I offered both the worlds
 to my love-stricken heart;
It considered all as passing,
 except your love.

Ḥâfeẓ

The army of your love sallied forth from an ambush
And launched a thousand tumults and disorders in
 the world.

'Erâqi

If you have not stolen the hearts of all the world
 with your flirtation,
Why have the hearts of all the world
 become smitten by your love?

'Erâqi

The way of love is easy and short in the end;
All ways other than this are long and drawn out.

'Erâqi

I've enjoyed a love above religion or unbelief,
I've enjoyed love without a trace of doubt or certitude.

'Aṭṭâr

For the lover, love builds Being in non-being;
The love based on existence is not Reality.

Sanâ'i

Love arrived and became like the blood in my veins and flesh
Until it emptied me of self and filled me with the friend.
All the limbs of my being became replete with the friend;
Only a name remains of me; the rest is all the friend.

Rumi

Love is that flame which, blazing up,
Burns everything other than the Beloved.

MM V 588

Love can't be confined to a collection of words;
Love does not belong to the realm of expression.
Whenever one's heart is devastated by love,
It can never thereafter recover.

'Aṭṭâr

Love is all burning and dissolving, nothing more;
It is nothingness and helplessness and need.
When love penetrates the breast,
The heart's blood seeps out through the eye.
Love does not go with lustful passion;
Love does not sit with ease and repose.

Neẓâmi

'Beauty' is said to represent the existence of all possible perfections gathered in one being, and this can apply only to God.

EE 55

In the absolute sense of the word, 'beauty' implies the 'essential beauty of the Divine Visage' *(wajh-e ḥaqq)*[2], but when it denotes 'relative beauty', subject to the conditions of creation, it refers to the harmonious proportions of the limbs of the physical body.

Beauty is a treasure, and the entire world its ruin;
Love is a mystery; the curtain of existence its veil.

TT 193

Your beauty and charm in harmony have seized
the world;
Indeed, through harmony, the entire world can
be seized.

Ḥâfeẓ

I have a fresh love from you at every moment;
You have, at every instant, a different beauty.

Ḥâfeẓ

His beauty is that which has no beginning;
My love is that which has no end.

Maghrebi

It is not surprising that the whole world is confounded
by you;
Since you are confounded by the reflection of your
own beauty.

Sa'di

1. *Ḥosn* signifies 'beauty' in the sense of 'virtue', 'goodness' or 'excellence' of character, as opposed to *jamâl,* which connotes 'beauty' as a reflection of the Divine Attribute, 'Beauty'.
2. See the author's *Sufi Symbolism* Vol. I (London: 1986) p.68.

Until your beauty gives light to our eyes,
We cannot observe your beauty's garden.

Rumi

'Beauty' is said to represent something which is pleasant in nature, such as 'elation' *(faraḥ)* or joyfulness, or an attribute of perfection, such as knowledge, or a praiseworthy trait, such as devotional practice. 'Beauty' is praiseworthy in the world and brings reward in the hereafter.

'Beauty' is of two kinds, the first, 'essential beauty' which is inherent in itself, such as having faith in God and His attributes, and the second, 'attributive beauty', which is applied to an attribute of something such as a 'holy war' *(jehâd)*, which is not beautiful in itself, because it involves the destruction of cities and the torment and killing of God's creatures. The Prophet said, "A human being is God's edifice, and he who destroys this edifice is accursed." However, the beauty in *jehâd* lies in the bearing of God's word aloft and the destruction of God's foes. This beauty exists for the combatting of unbelief.

TJ 59

'Beauty' *(ḥosn)* in any well-favoured man or woman is an expression of the Divine Beauty *(jamâl)*. As a reflection of the beauty of the Beloved, it is referred to as 'Divine Beauty' by the lovers, because the Beloved is only revealed through a given manifestation, and the manifestation can be attributed only to the Manifester.

RSh III 233

Know that 'beauty' is one of the Attributes of God and that is eternal *(qadim)*, for God's Essence is eternal. When God wishes to steal the heart of his devotee, he projects the lights of his beauty into the devotee's heart, and through His beauty pours the wine of 'loving-kindess' and 'love' therein. Love is increased as the viewing of beauty is increased for 'love' and 'loving-kindness' are closely related to the seeing of the Eternal Beauty. The beauty of God is His most particular attribute and is referred to in the verse: "So blessed be God, the finest of creators" (XXIII: 14), in which God, in creating that which is pleasing in His domain, describes Himself in terms of the manifestation of His beauty.

The lover of God, Moḥammad, received the grace of 'loving-kindness' through viewing God in the raiment of beauty, saying, "I have seen my Lord in the fairest of forms."[1] This station is not revealed to the devotee until he becomes accepted by the Eternal Beauty because of his sanctity and purification from what is transitory *(ḥawâdeth).* Once he attains this, he becomes the mirror of God's beauty in the world, like Adam, Joseph, Moses, Jesus and Moḥammad, who were the principle sources of beauty and who were graced with the pre-eternal beauty *(ḥosn-e azal)*, for God has revealed His Beauty through them and beauty has become their legacy to the possessors of beauty *(jamâl)* in this world and in the hereafter. They are the finest demonstrations of God's Beauty in the world. Consider the invocation of one gnostic: "O One whose beauty is the veil of His beauty."

'Beauty' is one of the characteristics of love in the lover, which God reveals to him only at the end of his journey towards Him. As his journey becomes completed in love, he sees nothing praiseworthy except by virtue of God's beauty within it. This is why the lover prefers 'virtuous beauty' *(ḥosn)* over all other forms of beauty in the realm of being.

According to a Tradition, the Prophet liked fair faces, saying that to look upon a lovely face increases one's visual faculty.[2]

Dho'n-Nun said, "Whoever gains intimacy with God, gains it with everything of charm and with every beautiful face."

The gnostic said, "Love and beauty are two eternal attributes which are never revealed exclusively of one another to the sincere devotee, because all attributes are interconnected." The relationship between love and beauty is indicated in the Koran, where God says to Moses: "And I endowed you with love from Me, so that you may be trained according to My view" (XX: 39). This passage has been interpreted as meaning "the beauty in Your eye is such that whoever sees You loves You."

MA 132

1. Although popular in Persian Sufism these traditions are absent from any of the orthodox compilations of prophetic traditions. See Schimmel, *Mystical Dimensions of Islam* (Chapel Hill: 1975) p.290.
2. Same as above.

THE MYSTERY-OF-BEAUTY *(ân)*

The 'mystery-of-beauty' is a particular quality of 'beauty' *(ḥosn);* it is indefinable and can be perceived only through 'spiritual tasting' *(dhauq)*.

In Sufi terminology the 'mystery-of-beauty' refers to 'love'.

KF 98

The mystery-of-beauty is a hidden subtlety
 from which beauty springs forth;
It cannot be described
 as a beloved's 'ruby lip' or 'down'.

Ḥâfeẓ

That which the Sufis call the mystery-of-beauty is you,
You who are the object of God's attention.
Like your Sufis, I call you the mystery-of-beauty;
But no! You are the very King of the mystery-of-beauty.
You are finer than Joseph, for you
Possess mystery-of-beauty, and he does not.

Sanâ'i

Seek the mystery-of-beauty from beautiful people,
 O heart, if you're a connoisseur of beauty;
This was said by one who had knowledge of vision.

Ḥâfeẓ

The Beloved is not one
 with beautiful hair and a slender waist;
Be the slave of that radiant face
 which has the mystery-of-beauty.

Ḥâfeẓ

LOVELINESS *(malâḥat)*

'Loveliness' is the appearance of Absolute Beauty which exhibits equilibrium and harmony in all its aspects. This beauty has many names, however, because of the differences in those manifestations. When it concerns beauty of human features and form, for example, it is referred to as 'loveliness', while when it concerns verbal expression, it is called 'lucidity' and 'eloquence', as Shabestari demonstrates in the following verse:

Loveliness emerged in the world
Without an equal, like a carefree *rend.*[1]
It raised its standards in the town of virtue;
It threw the whole world into confusion.

At times it rides proudly on the Rakhsh[2] of beauty;
At times wields its speech like a sharp blade.
In a person it is termed 'loveliness';
In speech it is called 'eloquence'.

TT 229

Your loveliness brought gladness
to the age of love;
Your subtlety brought fortune
to the time of beauty.

Ḥâfeẓ

'Loveliness' is said to represent the infinitude of divine perfections, the limits of which no one can be sure of reaching.

EE 55

Although those who show their beauty off
have been unveiled in full display,
No one matches our Beloved
in beauty or in loveliness.

Ḥâfeẓ

1. A *rend* may be described as one whose friendship with God is not dependent upon conventional means of behaviour or religious practice; on the contrary, his manner of approach may often offend those who claim piety and the ritual worship of God. See *Farhang-e Nurbakhsh* Vol 6, p. 162.
2. The horse of Rostam, Iran's legendary hero.

BELOVED *(maḥbub)*

The 'Beloved' is said to represent God, that is, he who is absolutely free of the need for 'friendship' *(dusti)*.

EE 54

You're the Beloved of my heart,
the ease of my soul: what can I do?
You're the ruler of all creatures
of the world: what can I do?

Shâh Ne'mato'llâh

The 'Beloved' signifies the reality *(ḥaqiqat)* of the spirit which is the essence of God.

KF 274

The 'Beloved' represents absolute Being or the 'Beauty of the Divine Visage' *(wajh-e ḥaqq)*, which is free of limitation or qualification.

Whatever the Beloved does, I do, for she is me
And I am she, though I am behind a veil.

TT 227

BELOVED *(ma'shuq)*

The 'Beloved' *(ma'shuq)*, is said to represent God in that he is the only one worthy of friendship from any point of view.

RA 42

Since the Beloved does not
remove the mask from her face,
Why does everyone insist
on guessing the nature of it?

Ḥâfeẓ

How can a heart without love discover the Beloved?
What has a soulless place to do with the Soul of Souls?

'Erâqi

Everyone calls his Beloved by a name;
My Beloved has no name.

Sa'di

Grasp the knocker on the Beloved's door
And dedicate there your grief-stricken soul.

'Aṭṭâr

Since the Beloved's visage has no parallel or likeness,
The King of Love has no beginning or end.

'Aṭṭâr

WITNESS *(shâhed)*[1]

The 'witness' represents that which appears in the heart as a result of either witnessing *(moshâhada)*, ecstasy, a mystical state, theophany or vision *(shohud)*.

The 'witness' is said to represent theophany.

EE 417

The 'witness' is that which appears after 'absence'; where God is the 'witness' in one's inner consciousness *(serr)*, the inner consciousness is that which is witnessed and when the gnostic is the 'witness', that which he perceives [God] is that which is witnessed.

SS 563

1. While this word denotes 'witness' or 'beholder', it has also come to connote the Beloved, inspiring contemplation or reflection of the divine beauty. In Arabic, *shâhed* is an active participle meaning 'witness', 'viewer', or 'subject' of contemplation; its plural is *shawâhed*, 'witnesses' (proofs). The verbal noun is *shohud*, meaning 'being a witness', from which a further verbal nominal form *moshâhada* ('witnessing', 'contemplative vision', 'visionary experience') is derived. The word *mashhud* is the passive participle, meaning 'that which is seen or witnessed', the 'Object of contemplation' (God). In the state of *shohud* (vision) both the *shâhed* and the *mashhud* merge into one.

The lover possessing pure inner consciousness describes, in terms of the transitory, his vision of different aspects of the Eternal, as the 'witness'. The masters say that the 'witness' is present, and whatever is present in your heart is your witness.

The gnostic said, "The 'witness' experiences visionary revelation *(mokâshafa)* of mysteries at the sight of 'lights'." This is the meaning of the Prophet's words: "The 'witness' sees that which the absent one does not see."[1]

MA 123

The 'witness' represents the appearance of the absolute beauty in descending levels of existence or in the objects in which theophany is displayed.

Wine, candle and witness:
all of them are present;
Do not become distracted;
pay attention to the witness.

TT 208

The term 'witness' refers to that which appears in the heart as a result of contemplative vision*(moshâhada)*. This 'witness' is endowed with its own peculiar traits, which attest to the validity of the Object of contempation *(al-mashhud)*. The 'witness' could be either in the form of infused knowledge *('elm-e ladoni)*, or in the form of a state, a theophany, or contemplative vision.

ES 153

The word 'witness' connotes 'that which is present' and in Sufi terminology it signifies something which is present in the heart of a person, the remembrance of which dominates the heart. If it is knowledge which prevails in the heart, the heart is the 'witness of knowledge'; if it is ecstasy, then the heart is the 'witness of ecstasy'; and if it is God, the heart is the 'witness of God'.

TJ 83-84

1. Cited in Aḥmad ebn Hanbal's collection of *ḥadith: Mosnad* I:83; Wensinck: *Concordance de la tradition Musulmane* (Leiden: Brill, 1936) Vol. III, 190.

From the point of view of the wayfarers, the 'witness' is said to be God, in the sense of His being manifested and present in the form of things, as indicated by the name 'the Outward' *(aẓ-ẓâher)* (Koran LVII: 3). Conventionally, the 'witness' is said to be 'a person who is fair of form and feature.'

KF 738

Listen to me and focus your heart
On the witness whose beauty requires no adornment.

Ḥâfeẓ

Wine, candle, and witness are the essence
of the spiritual reality
Which is God's theophany in every form.

Shabestâri

Drunkenness from the eye of my cherished witness
is fine;
That's why my self-control has been given over
to drunkenness!

Ḥâfeẓ

WANTON WITNESS *(shâhed-e har-jâ'i)*

The 'Wanton Witness' is said to represent God.

O Lord, to whom may this point be made?
That the wanton one
Has not revealed its features
to anyone in the world.

Ḥâfeẓ

To whom may these words be addressed?
"My Beloved is the wanton witness
And is hidden behind a veil."

Sabzawâri

In the *Farhang-e Mo'âyana, mashhud* is defined as that which is the object of direct observation.

Since the light of our Prophet
  is both 'beholder' and 'beheld',
Surely it is the object
  of our vision throughout the world.

Shâh Ne'mato'llâh

The whole world is the mirror of his beautiful face.
Indeed there is nothing beheld in the world but him.

Lâhiji

That which is 'witnessed' *(al-mashhud)* by the lover is the permanence of the breaths of the holy spirits in the vistas of pre-eternal proximity. So sublime becomes the lover's state at this sight that the divine word applies to him, whereof God testifies to the two conditions experienced by the lover, saying: "By the Witness and the Witnessed" (LXXXV: 3).

Wâseṭi said, "The witness is God, and the witnessed is creation."

Jonaid said, "The witness is God, who is aware and cognisant of both your consciousness and your unconsciousness."

Sarrâj said, "The witnessed is what the witness sees."

The gnostic said, "Whenever his time *(waqt)*[1] dictates intoxication *(sokr)*, the 'witness' is the gnostic himself, but when conditions necessitate sobriety *(ṣaḥw)*, the 'witness' becomes the Object of gnosis. When the 'witness' is God, the witnessed is the devotee, but when the witness becomes the devotee, the witnessed is God."

MA 124

WITNESSED, WITNESS, WITNESSES, AND CONTEMPLATIVE VISION *(mashhud, shâhed, shawâhed wa shohud)*

The Sufis refer to the 'witness' as the 'witnessed' in the sense that

1. See the author's *Spiritual Poverty in Sufism* (London: 1984) p. 93

whenever the heart is in the the presence of something, that thing is correspondingly in the presence of the heart. Furthermore, wherever the term *shâhed* ('witness') is employed in the singular, 'God' is meant, and wherever it is employed in the plural *shawâhed* ('witnesses'), the 'creation' is meant, connoting the 'Unity of God' and the 'multiplicity of the creation'. When the term 'contemplative vision' is employed, 'presence with God' is meant, where the heart is the constant 'witness' of and constantly in the presence of God.

MH 141

HEART-HOLDER *(deldâr)*

The 'heart-holder' is said to represent the attribute of expansion which brings 'joy' *(sorur)* and 'loving-kindness' to the heart.

EE 58

The heart is becoming devastated;
make the heart-holder aware!
Take care, O friends;
by your souls, look after my soul!

Ḥâfeẓ

The intellect has gone crazy;
where is that musky chain of tresses?
The heart is in retreat from me;
where is that heart-holder's eyebrow?

Ḥâfeẓ

Since the illuminated see the mirror of the heart
as being clear,
They can see the heart-holder's face reflected clearly
in that mirror.

'Erâqi

My drunken heart like a bird half-dead
Has fallen into the trap of a heart-holder like you.

'Aṭṭâr

 The term 'heart-holder' refers to the realm of 'contemplative vision', (that is to say, of 'witnessing' the essence of God).

KF 1557

The 'heart-holder' is said to symbolise the divine attribute of expansion *(basṭ)*, engendered in the lover's heart by the radiant effulgence *(lawâme')* of 'loving-kindness' and the blazing fire of 'yearning' *(shauq)* and 'ardent love' *(mawaddat),* in such a way that the determined form of the lover vanishes like a particle in the sun of the beauty of the Beloved, causing the light of the lover's existence to become diffused amongst the principal essences.

The heart-holder has vexed my heart;
what consolation!
Through a hundred kinds of grief she debases me;
what sympathy!

TT 196-197

HEART-RAVISHER *(delbar)*

The 'heart-ravisher' is said to represent the attribute of contraction engendered in the heart through 'anguish' *(anduh)* and 'tribulation' *(meḥnat).*

EE 58

Although she knew my heart
was in distress,
The heart-ravisher did not consider
the moment right for comfort.

Ḥâfeẓ

Whatever we want to do,
the heart-ravisher wants something different;
That which the ravisher does
is that which we shall do.

'Erâqi

Draw me away from myself, O heart-ravisher,
For there is no other veil before me
than that of myself.

Maghrebi

How long this unremitting
indifference, O heart-ravisher?
How long this unrelieved
affliction, O heart-ravisher?

Sanâ'i

The 'heart-ravisher' is said to symbolise the attribute of contraction, engendered by the appearance of 'loving-kindness' and the presence of 'love' in the heart of the lover.

I have a heart ravisher who is my confidante;
She is my companion in this world and the next.

TT 196

SOUL-MATE *(jânân)*[1]

'Soul-mate' represents the attribute of self-subsistence *(qayyum)* by the grace of which all things exist.

EE 58

Don't ask why;
the fortunate devotee
Accepts with all his soul whatever
his soul-mate should say.

Ḥâfeẓ

When lovers knock with fervour
on the door of the heart,
They set the love-crazed heart
afire with fervour for the soul-mate.

'Erâqi

1. Lit 'souls', pl. of *jân* soul.

The 'friend' is said to represent the divine loving-kindness which precedes that of the wayfarers.

EE 41

The delightful moments were those
which were spent with the friend;
The rest were all unrewarding
and uninspired.

Ḥâfeẓ

Although the friend would not
pay anything for us,
We wouldn't exchange a single hair from her head
for all the world.

Ḥâfeẓ

Heaven full of milk, honey and wine
is but a barren waste for us
Without the beauty of the friend.

'Erâqi

The 'friend' is said to signify the theophany of the Attributes of God displayed to the spirit.

LG II 2

COMPANION *(yâr)*

The 'companion' is said to represent the Divine attribute which is necessary for the existence of all created things; there is no name of God more favourable to the wayfarer, for it pertains to the term, 'divine unity' *(tauḥid)*.

EE 41

The companion is with us:
    what need have we to seek for more?
It's enough for our soul
    to associate with that intimate one.

Ḥâfeẓ

First I shook the world from my skirts,
Then sincerely seized the skirts of the companion.

Maghrebi

We are constantly in pain; there is no relief.
O for the dust of the companion's doorway!

Aṭṭâr

The 'companion' is said to refer to the realm of 'vision' *(shohud)* that is to say, the 'contemplative vision' *(moshâhada)* of the Divine Essence.

KF 1564

MISTRESS, BELOVED *(negâr)*[1]

The 'mistress' is said to represent God and also to refer to the perfect master, who is the manifestation of God's attributes.

O mistress, the time has come for you
    to be my companion for one moment;
My heart has grown weary with itself;
    come and be my soul.

'Erâqi

O mistress, my heart is filled with images;
Strip these images from my heart, O Beloved!

Maghrebi

1. *Negâr* literally means: a 'picture', 'painting', 'portrait', 'image'.

O mistress, how long must you cause
this yearning heart to suffer?
Or is it unthinkable for you
to provide well-being to lovers?

Sanâ'i

In that meadow where idols
seize the hands of lovers,
If it is no trouble,
O please be my mistress!

Ḥâfeẓ

THE SOUGHT *(maṭlub)*

The 'sought' is said to symbolise the Divine Aspect *(wajh-e ḥaqq)* at all spiritual levels of the heart.

The truth is, that when one seeks someone,
That sought one's soul seeks him.

TT 228

The 'sought' is said to refer to God for the seeker who lacks the capacity for 'friendship' *(dusti)* with Him.

EE 54

With respect to the 'witness' and the 'witnessed',
You are observer and observed;
With respect to the 'lover' and 'beloved',
You're the seeker and the sought.

Maghrebi

'Aṭṭâr, you are drunk with love;
How long will you boast about it?
If you're a seeker, become annihilated;
The sought is obvious enough!

'Aṭṭâr

Don't search here and there for the intended object
Of both worlds — the Sought of the universe:
Do your seeking in your soul!

Rumi

The terms 'seeker' *(ṭâleb)* and 'sought' *(maṭlub)* have also been applied to the disciple and master, where the 'seeker' may be defined as the one who searches for Reality *(ḥaqiqat)*, in order to find it, and the 'sought' is the one whom Reality seeks in order to bestow intimacy with itself upon him.

BELOVED *(ḥabib)*

Ḥabib is said to represent both the Beloved and the lover. In Sufi terminology this is generally used to represent the Beloved who is God. When representing the lover, it is one of the Prophet's sobriquets, 'lover of God' *(ḥabibo'llâh)*.

It is better to keep your sadness for the Beloved
from the eyes of the envious,
For one who harbours spite
cannot keep a secret.

Ḥâfeẓ

Do not seek the cure for heartache from a doctor;
It can be cured only by the Beloved's sweet scent.

'Erâqi

When a ray of the Beloved's beauty
shone upon my heart,
The eye of the soul saw the beauty
in the perfection of 'God's lover'.

Maghrebi

INTIMATE FRIEND *(khalil)*

Abraham was called the 'intimate friend' of God *(Khalilo'llâh)*, because he had embraced and penetrated all the attributes of the divine essence, just as colour permeates all that is coloured. Can you not see how God is manifested through the attributes of relative beings, and do you not see how created being is manifested through God's attributes? Know that whenever something is permeated by something else it is assumed into the other. That which permeates, the agent, is disguised by that which is permeated, the object of permeation.

If God is considered as the 'Outwardly Manifest' *(aẓ-ẓâher)*, and the creature as being hidden in Him, the creature will assume all the names of God: God's hearing and sight, all His relationships [modes], and His knowledge. (This is called the 'station of nearness resulting from observance of prescribed religious duties', *qorb-e farâ'eḍh)*. If however, the creature is considered to be manifest, God will be hidden in him as the 'Inward' *(al-bâṭen)*, becoming his hearing, sight, hand, foot and all his faculties. This is called the 'station of nearness resulting from supererogatory practice' *(qorb-e nawâfel)*,[1] to which the well known Tradition of the Prophet attests.[2]

FH I 80-81

The prophet Abraham was given the sobriquet *Khalilo'llâh* because God penetrated every limb of his body, assuming his form, such that every action that he performed and every characteristic that he displayed came from God for Abraham did not exist apart from God.

From another point of view, Abraham permeated all of God's manifestations. After becoming annihilated from himself, he became subsistent *(qâ'em)* in God, such that he witnessed in himself all the attributes of the Divine Essence. Just as the Divine Identity *(howiyat)* permeates all things, so Abraham was permeated by the Divine Identity due to the union of personification and appearance. Therefore, all the attributes ascribed to the Divine Essence were witnessed in Abraham.

SGR 263

1. See the author's *Traditions of the Prophet* Vol. I p. 14-15.
2. Adapted with minor changes from R.W.J. Austin's translation of *Ibn al-'Arabi: The Bezels of Wisdom*, p. 91-2 (Pub. by The Missionary Society of St. Paul the Apostle, New York 1980; Paulist Press and the SPCK, London).

O Lord, make cold this fire in my soul,
Just as you did for your friend.[1]

Ḥâfeẓ

THE DIFFERENCE BETWEEN THE LOVER AND INTIMATE FRIEND *(farq bain-e ḥabib wa khalil)*

When Nuri was asked which was higher, 'God's lover' *(ḥabib)*[2] or 'God's friend' *(khalil)*, he said, "God's friend is one who submits, because he is called upon to do so, whereas God's lover submits to God of his own accord."

TS(S) 153

The 'friend' is the disciple and the 'lover' is the master. The disciple is the desirer and the master the desired [by God]. The disciple goes by himself and the master is taken. The 'friend' stands amongst those who serve in the court of Lordship *(robubiyat)*, while the 'lover' sits amongst the 'near ones' *(nazdikân)* in the presence of the Oneness *(aḥadiyat)*. 'Oneness' is the place of those who are taken, while Lordship is the station of those who go.

KAM I 367

Wâseṭi describes the difference as follows: "The 'friend' goes from the creation to God, while the 'lover' comes from God to the creation. The former knows God through proofs, while the latter knows proofs through God."

KAM VIII 299

LOVER *(moḥebb)*

The 'lover' *(moḥebb)* is said to be the one who has 'loving-kindness' towards God, whether it is associated with seeking or not; it may involve seeking at one point and not at another.

EE 54

1. Abraham. This is a reference to Koran XXI: 69.
2. *Ḥabib* is a sobriquet for Moḥammad; as stated earlier it can mean 'lover' as well as 'beloved'. See p. 45.

The lover never speaks of his pain to a physician;
He who complains about pain from the Beloved
has no real pain.

Kamâl Khojandi

In our creed, the lover
and the loved are one.
In desire, desirer
and desired are one.

Shâh Ne'mato'llâh

How long will your tongue flicker on like a candle?
The moth-like beloved has arrived; hush now, O lover!

Ḥâfeẓ

Ebn 'Aṭâ' said, "The life of the lover is in the heart. The life or the yearning one, in tears. The life of the gnostic, in remembrance. The life of the unitarian, in speech. The life of the reverent one in the breath. The life of the man of aspiration in disassociation from the *nafs*, and this latter means to be burned up and drowned.

TA 493

LOVER *('âsheq)*

The 'lover' is said to be the one who searches for God with intense effort and complete 'friendship'.

EE 54

Where is there a better lover of you than I,
that you should be involved with him?
Where is there a better heart ravisher for me than you,
that I should be involved with her?

Maghrebi

In what creed do they do this?
    In what cult do they do this?
Where do they kill a lover
    asking, "Why are you my lover?"

'Erâqi

Lovers drunkenly place their intellects
    in their sleeves, and their souls in their hands;
They ride towards him on the Buraq[1] of their heart
    and cast off all that they have at his feet.

Sanâ'i

SEEKER *(ṭâleb)*

The 'seeker' is said to be both searcher and petitioner. In Sufi terminology, he is described as someone in pain, searching for Reality. He is someone who has not yet submitted to a master, but is looking for a spiritual guide to lead him to Reality.

The 'seeker' is said to be the one who seeks the truth through devotion and adoration of perfection, rather than by way of love or friendship.

EE54

There was no seeking of him,
    till seeking came from him;
All this searching of ours
    comes from his searching [for us].

Maghrebi

We are seekers of your face,
    wandering adrift in your lane;
Show your visage, O chosen
    heart-ravisher of ours!

Rumi

1. The steed on which Moḥammad rode during his *mer'âj,* (noctural journey).

In the terminology of the wayfarers, the 'seeker' is one who passes from instinctual appetites and desires of the *nafs* to the point where he may lift the veil of imagination from the face of Reality and go from multiplicity to Unity in order to become a perfect human being. This station is known as 'annihilation in God' *(fanâ' fe'llâh),*[1] and is the final station on the path of the 'seekers'.

KF 900

UNION *(waṣl, weṣâl)*

'Union' is said to represent the wayfarer's arrival at the station of True Unity *(waḥdat-e ḥaqiqi)* once he has abandoned the transitory ego.

Everyone seeks to taste
 the food of union,
But who will have the fortune
 to sit at the table?

Kamâl Khojandi

What is union?
To come into being from non-existence,
And to emerge drunk from both.

MN 42

The proper gratitude for the unveiling of the day of union
Is to forget the complaint of the night of separation.

Ḥâfeẓ

I draw life from the hope of union with you;
Otherwise how could I bear separation?

'Erâqi

1. For acomplete discussion of fanâ', see the authors, *Sufism: Fear and Hope*, New York: 1982.

How may I seek union with you,
when it does not come through seeking?
How may I describe you,
when speech comes not to my tongue?

'Aṭṭâr

'Union' is said to represent the station of unity with God, both inwardly and outwardly.

EE 69

'Union' is said to symbolise the attainment of unity, the Oneness of Concentration *(aḥadiyato'l-jam'),* and the nearness referred to in the *ḥadith,* "I have a time with God,"[1] due to the annihilation of habitual practices and the shedding of all attributes of creation.

According to Shabestari:

Union with God is separation from creation;
Acquaintanceship with God is estrangement from oneself.

TT 235

'Union' is said to represent true unity, which is the link between outward and inward being. It also signifies annihilation of the wayfarer in the Attributes of God, and the realisation of the Divine Names.

Moreover, 'union' is said to mean that one is not, even for a moment, separated from God; the tongue is occupied in remembrance, the heart in reflection; and the soul in the witnessing of God, being with Him in all states. The one in 'union' is said to be one who is liberated from himself and joined with God, becoming characterised by His qualities and devoid of any trace of personal identity, like a drop vanishing into the sea.

KF 1503

Ebn Khafif said, "Union is to be joined with the Beloved and absent from all things but God."

TA 578

1. Cf. *Traditions of the Prophet,* Vol.I, p. 31-32.

BEHOLDING *(didâr)*

'Beholding' is said to symbolise the seeing of God with the eye of the heart. It also symbolises the seeing of the perfect guide or the Beloved with both the inward and outward eye.

Our ship is broken; spring up, O favourable wind,
So that we may behold the beloved once again!

Ḥâfeẓ

Like Jacob, I cry out with piteous grief,
For my desire is to behold Canaan's beautous Joseph.

Rumi

What is a hundred years of suffering
When you behold the beloved for a day?

KAM VII 513

'Love' *(mehr)* and 'Beholding' once encountered one another.

'Love' said, " 'Beholding', you are like the light which illumines the world."

'Beholding' said, " 'Love', you are like a fire which consumes the world. When I unveil, I root out all sadness from the heart."

'Love' said, "I cultivate the heart in which I take up residence."

'Beholding' said, "I am the gift to those who are tested."

'Love' said, "I agitate the world."

KAM III 639

KISS *(bus, busa)*

The 'kiss' is said to symbolise the ability to comprehend the subtlety of discourse, whether scientific or practical, inward or outward.

EE 69

The 'kiss' is said to symbolise the inner grace and attraction that comes from God to the wayfarer. It may also represent sensual pleasure.

KF 1553

Beholding is within reach,
    as are the kiss and embrace;
I am grateful for my fortune
    and the course of events.

Ḥâfeẓ

I snatched a kiss from your lips;
    my heart sought another.
Estrangement from you said,
    "Go away, there is no more."

'Erâqi

I fear you will die of joy
    at the moment of the kiss;
O soul do not ask of the lip
    whose threshold is this!

Kamâl Khojandi

EMBRACE *(kenâr)*[1]

The 'embrace' symbolises the taking of the true Beloved *(ma'shuq-e ḥaqiqi)* into one's arms, in the form of constant remembrance *(dhekr)*, reflection *(fekr)*, continuous contemplation *(morâqaba)* and perception of the mysteries.

Why drive away a broken one like me?
My only wish is for a kiss or an embrace.

Ḥâfeẓ

The 'embrace' is said to symbolise the reception of the mysteries of 'divine unity' *(tauḥid)* and continous contemplation.[2]

KF 1561

Unless, like desire, you come into my embrace,
No aim of mine will be realised.

Kamâl Khojandi

1. Cf. *âghush, Sufi Symbolism,* Vol. I, p. 12-13.
2. Cf. EE 69.

CLOSENESS *(nazdiki)*

'Closeness' is said to symbolise awareness through gnosis of the divine means, attributes, and acts.

EE 71

Do not go away, dear one;
come, sit down close to me.
Why wander, aimless like a stranger?
You have the mark of aquaintance.

Shâh Ne'mato'llâh

Though far from my eye,
you are close to my heart,
Since you are ever
in the thoughts of my heart.

'Erâqi

Bâyazid said, "Those persons farthest from God's court are those who imagine they are closest to God."

NO 123

DISTANCE *(duri)*

'Distance' is to be aware of all knowledge, qualities and nuances related to the realm of dispersion.

EE 71

An instant's distance from the friend's lane
Is prohibited in the lovers creed.

Rumi

Whoever, like 'Erâqi,
is distant from the friend,
Has eyes full of tears
and a burning heart.

'Erâqi

In Sufi terminology, 'separation' represents separation from the station of Unity.

'Separation' is said to symbolise attention to what is other than God, whether inwardly or outwardly.[1]

KF 1532

'Separation' is said to symbolise the heart's attention and focusing upon that which is other than the true sought one *(maṭlub-e ḥaqiqi)*[2], whether inwardly or outardly.

Go away, ascetic, from the drunkard's lane!
We are men of union; speak not of separation!

TT 236

After the union which passed like the wind,
Alas! this sadness separation came in.

'Aṭṭâr

Because the sadness of separation has arrived,
We have been beaten to the ground.
Since we lost the cure, we have died in pain.

Ḥâfeẓ

I find no union with her;
My body is in separation from her.
Since I'm not worthy of happiness,
Misery has taken precedence.

'Erâqi

Union and separation are the speciality of lovers.
If you're a gnostic, Maghrebi,
Shut up about union and separation!

Maghrebi

1. Cf. EE 69.
2. See also *maṭlub*, p. 44.

In the terminology of the lovers, 'estrangement' signifies the separation of the lover from the Beloved.

'Estrangement' is said to represent absence from the station of unity *(waḥdat)*.

EE 69

In normal usage *ferâq* means simply separation from a person, whereas in Sufi terminology, when the lover becomes separated from his Beloved for but a moment, he undergoes a 'hundred-year estrangement'. The movement of the wayfarer away from his origin, which is the realm of the inward, to the realm of the outward, is called the wayfarer's 'estrangement'. By the same token, the return from the realm of the outward to that of the inward is known as the wayfarer's union and can be attained only through physical death.

KF 1130

One of the stations of those who experience yearning for God is 'estrangement'.

The reality of the 'First Transcendence' *(tanzih-e awwal)*[1] causes total 'estrangement' of all that is other than God from the vistas of perception of union with Eternity, this in itself being 'estrangement' from the cognition of the Essence. Since the Divinity cannot be perceived, known or qualified by a created being, how is it possible that essential oneness *(aḥadiyat)* be perceived by that which has been created?

Praise be to God! There is neither cause nor relation between God and creation, "...they cannot encompass it in knowledge" (Koran XX: 110). Praise be to God, that in his essence he made no one person exempt from this estrangement, commiting all to the fire of estrangement and veiling them from the meaning of his majesty.

The Sufis have said that 'estrangement' is the result of an error on the part of the Sufi which causes him to be subjected to the trial of separation and distress. Such a person is veiled from the contemplation *(moshâhada)* of nearness *(qorb)* because of his personal characteristics. However, such estrangement never occurs unless the mystic is presented with the reality of gnosis and the theophany of eternity and witnesses the invalidation of his own

1. *Tanzih* refers to God's absolute trancendence which allows for no relationship or comparison with creation at all.

[temporal] gnosis. Thus, God, because of His jealousy and the mystic's increased gnosis of nearness to Him, veils the gnostic. He is veiled by God's beauty from God's beauty, and by God's majesty from God's majesty. God, thus, dissolves the gnostic's spirit in yearning and annihilates his inner consciousness in love.

Can one not see the dignity displayed by Adam in this state, how he ate the grain of wheat?[1]. Or Noah's state when he beseeched God to save his son?[2] Or note the Prophet's words, "Such a darkness descends upon my heart that I beseech God's forgiveness seventy times a day."[3]

It has been said that 'estrangement' is a major occurrence which befalls any great, spiritual liberated human being.

The gnostic said, "Estrangement is a flame of the fire of divine jealousy which flares up from the tinder box of the divine glory."

MA 106-107

'Estrangement' is said to symbolise 'distance' *(bo'd)* and 'separation' of the *nafs* from the sanctum of the Essential Unity *(waḥdat-e dhâti)* and the Unseen Divine Identity *(howiyat-e ghaib)*. Ḥâfeẓ writes:

I once heard these fine words
 from the master of Canaan.[4]
"Estrangement from the friend
 is so painful it cannot be described."

TT 219

Dho'n-Nun Meṣri said, "Know that fear of estrangement compared to the fear of the fire is as a drop of water cast into a mighty ocean. Indeed, I know of nothing more heart-gripping than fear of estrangement."

TA 150

1. Koran II: 35, VII: 20, XX: 120. The wheat or barley that Adam ate, thereby causing his expulsion from paradise, is represented by the apple in Christian theology.
2. Koran XI: 42.
3. See the author's *Traditions of the Prophet,* Vol. I p. 38.
4. Jacob.

My inclination is toward union,
her intention is my estrangement;
I've abandoned my own wish,
so that the beloved's wish will be fulfilled.

Ḥâfeẓ

Those subjected to tribulation
through sadness and anguish of estrangement
Again find their hearts ablaze like the fire-temple
and their eyes awash like the sea.

'Erâqi

Like your tumbling tresses,
falling in every direction,
Those who are slaughtered by you
have fallen into estrangement.

'Aṭṭâr

SADNESS *(ghamm)*

'Sadness' is said to represent diligent commitment in seeking the Beloved.

EE 69

'Sadness' is said to symbolise complete diligence on the part of the lover in seeking presence and union with the Beloved, such that this 'sadness' becomes intimate with his estranged heart and reminds him of his Beloved.

Loneliness drove my anguished heart to despair;
If sadness for her had not been my intimate,
what would I have done?

TT 218

Abu 'Othmân was once asked, "What is the sadness that one experiences without knowing its origin?" He replied, "The spirit records the sins and crimes of the *nafs,* while the *nafs* forgets them. When the spirit encounters an awakened *nafs*, it presents the sins and crimes of the *nafs* to it, whereby the *nafs* becomes humbled and ashamed. This is the sadness which one experiences without knowing its origin."

LT 226

The burden of sadness
    had sickened my heart;
Then God sent one with a Jesus-breath,[1]
    who caused it to disappear.

Ḥâfeẓ

With all of these cares,
    sadness for you is still
Finer for me than a thousand joys.

'Erâqi

Gladness of union for the soul
    will one day come from the soul of souls
To the one whose heart harbours
    the sadness of love.

Rumi

Wherever 'I' am, there is sadness and no heart;
Wherever you are, there is heart and no sadness.

Sanâ'i

HOME OF SADNESS *(ghammkada)*

The 'home of sadness' is said to represent the station of being veiled.[2]

KF 1560

1. See the author's *Jesus in the Eyes of Sufis,* (London: 1983) p. 52.
2. Cf. EE 70

The 'consoler' is said to symbolise God's merciful attribute *(ṣefat-e raḥmâni)* which encompasses all people.

EE 58

If I complain of that ruby lip
which tortures my heart with its amorous gestures,[1]
You will be my consoler.

Ḥâfeẓ

Though the lover had nothing but a sad soul
He immediately offered it up as a gift to the consoler.

Kamâl Khojandi

'Consolation' is said to symbolise the attribute of Mercy, the favour of which brings benefit to all beings.

What a favoured time it is
when the companion[2] arrives.
Consolation has come to fulfill
the wishes of the sad ones.

TT 219

'Consolation' symbolises the effect of the attribute of Beauty *(ṣefat-e jamâli)*, which encompasses all people.

KF 1540

Where is that intimate,
that consoler of the soul?
Where is that witness
of the soul of every being?

'Erâqi

1. *Eshwa* p. 125
2. *Yar* p. 42

You left and sadness remained in my heart;
    O that you might return
And I could recount each sadness of heart
    to such a consoler as you.

Hâtef Eṣfahâni

O my lips, be silent!
    listen to the beautiful mistress[1]
So that through her grace
    she may give that rare consolation.

Rumi

SYMPATHISER *(ghammkhwâr)*

The 'sympathiser' is said to represent God's compassionate attribute *(ṣefat-e raḥimi),* which is particular to certain people.

EE 58

Every day these demons inflict
    sadness a hundred times over:
O misery! That with all this sadness
    the consoler is not in sight.

'Aṭṭâr

If he'd be my friend
    I'd not be left friendless;
If he's my sympathiser,
    I shall not be sad.

'Erâqi

The 'sympathiser' is said to symbolise the compassionate attribute of God, which is experienced only by those who enjoy felicity[2] and those who attain good fortune in the hereafter.

1. *Negâr*, p. 43.
2. *Sa'âdat*, p. 93

Be aware that the link with life
is no more than a hair's-breadth;
Keep your sympathising for yourself,
don't waste it on the world.

TT 218-219

CONCERN *(hamm)*

The conventional meaning for the word *hamm* can mean 'aim' and 'intention' or 'anguish' and 'depression'.

It differs from 'sadness' in that sadness suggests anguish over the past, while 'concern' implies anguish for the future.

In Sufi terminology, 'concern' is said to represent the complete attention of the Sufi in seeking God...

'Concern' is said to symbolise the lover's aim and effort in the seeking of the Beloved, in such a way that the heart is occupied only with this seeking.

TT 236

In Sufi terminology 'concern' is said to represent the gathering of all aspirations into a single collected 'concern'.

Abu Sa'id Kharrâz said, "Unify your concern before God."

Some have said that the devotee's 'concern' must be trampled under his feet, meaning that he should have no concern for past or future, and must be in the immediate present with his spiritual moment *(waqt)*.

LT 355

'Concern' is an allusion to the integration of all efforts into one. The reality of it embraces 'sorrow' *(ḥozn)* in the lover's heart, such that his inner consciousness desires union.

"She truly desired[1] him and he would have desired her..." (Koran XII: 24). Despite Joseph's firm rejection, Zolaikha, moved by an irresistable desire, still persisted in her efforts to be united with him.

SS 575

1. *Hamm.*

SOLE CONCERN *(hamm-e mofrad)*

'Sole concern' is that which is not commingled with consciousness of the transitory *(ḥadath).*

SS 568

Whenever the gnostic finds himself at the site of detachment from the world, his 'concern' becomes directed towards Uniqueness *(waḥdâniyat)*; that is to say, he desires Uniqueness alone, where neither 'concern' for veiling nor 'concern' for the transitory remains in him, as his 'aspiration' is directed towards the Lordship.

The gnostic said, " 'Sole concern' is only for those who have attained the station of Uniqueness."

MA 280

THE DIFFERENCE BETWEEN CONCERN AND ASPIRATION *(farq bain-e hamm wa hemmat)*

Abu 'Ali Daqqâq said, "When the disciple lacks 'concern' in the early stages and 'aspiration' in the final ones, he becomes idle. 'Concern' is that which engages one's outer being in devotional practice, while 'aspiration' is that which concentrates one's inner being in meditation."

TA 653

ASPIRATION *(hemmat)*

'Aspiration' represents attention of the heart and inclination of all the spiritual faculties towards God, in order to attain perfection for oneself or someone else.

TJ 320

There are three stages of 'aspiration', which arise from awakening, devotion *(erâdat)*, and Divine Reality *(ḥaqiqat).*

The 'aspiration arising from awakening' involves detaching the heart from all wishes, whether those wishes be realisable or not. The one who experiences this 'aspiration' must consider whether his wish is logically attainable. If it is, then he may proceed.

The 'aspiration arising from devotion' represents the beginning of the disciple's sincerity and is the 'concentration of aspiration'.

When it becomes concentrated,
It affects the world and its qualities.

It is said that the 'aspiration' of great men uproots mountains.

The 'aspiration arising from Divine Reality' is the concentration of all aspirations through the purity of divine inspiration. This is the 'committed aspiration' particular to the great masters amongst the people of God, who retire from multiplicity and seek Oneness *(aḥadiyat),* in order to attain divine unity *(tauḥid).*

RSh II 249

The one who does not fall short in his aspiration
Will, in the end, reach his lofty stature.

Ḥâfeẓ

AWAKENED ASPIRATION *(hemmato'l-efâqat)*

The 'awakened aspiration' is the first degree of 'aspiration' on the spiritual path, bringing about the search for that which is subsistent and the abandoning of that which is perishable.

Give up what is passing for that which is lasting,
So that you may become a wise man with insight.

RSh IV 26[1]

VAIN ASPIRATION *(hemmato'l-anafat)*

'Vain aspiration' is the second degree of 'aspiration'. The thoughts of the one who experiences this 'aspiration' are focused on reward for good works, his heart being engaged in expectation of the merit which God has promised as the result of right actions. In any case, he does not seek to witness God, but rather to worship God, in the hope of His beneficence. In his attention to God he seeks nearness to him, and does not seek that which is other that God.[2]

Let us not seek from him that which is other than him,
For if we seek other than him, we do not do well.

RSh IV 26

1. Cf. EE 45.
2. *Ibid.*

SUBLIME ASPIRATION *(hemmat arbâb al-hemam al-'âliyat)*[1]

'Sublime aspiration' is the third degree of 'aspiration'. This lofty degree is reached by those who are attached to nothing other than God, who pay no attention to what is other than him and who are not content with states or stations or lingering at the Names and Attributes; they focus only on the Essence itself.[2]

RSh IV 26

'Sublime aspiration' of the gnostic follows elation in God *(faraḥ)*.

God manifests himself in His attribute of favour and displays His beneficence to the gnostic, seeking to gain his heart and train him. At this point, the gnostic, experiencing expansion, realises his position and streams of eternal grace burst forth for him. However, he is not satisfied with this and he seeks more than this capacity allows, And says, "My Lord, increase my knowledge" (XX: 114). Ḥallâj said, "The sublime aspiration is where the gnostic is content only with annihilation in the eternal and attainment of subsistence after non-existence."

MA 140

DEPRESSION *(afsordagi)*

'Depression' is said to symbolise the prevailing coldness of the water element in nature which dampens the fire of yearning for divine gnosis.

How long will depression possess you,
And a hundred worlds of dying oppress you?

TT 171

Although love is all mercy and right guidance,
It will not come to every heart which is depressed.

Rumi

1. Literally the 'aspiration of the Masters of sublime aspiration'.
2. Cf. EE 46.

It is said that 'anguish' is the bewilderment which occurs in a state of inward spiritual motion.

LG II 6

'Anguish' is the wayfarer's bewilderment with respect to an occurrence on the path, where he is confounded by the circumstances of its arrival to him or departure from him.

While I was in anguish for you
I suffered a different pain at every moment.

TT 173[1]

Your lovers buy the anguish of your
Immortal love with their souls.

Sanâ'i

Beshr Ḥâfi said, "Anguish is a monarch who, once established, allows no one else to share his rule."

TA 134

Ebn Khafif said, "Anguish keeps the body from joy *(ṭarab).*"

TA 578

Abo'l-Ḥasan Kharaqâni said, "When God apportioned things amongst mankind, he bestowed anguish upon the *javânmardân*[2], and they accepted it." When asked how 'anguish' was acquired he said, "God's anguish will overcome you when, having striven wholeheartedly to proceed in purity on His path, you look within yourself and find that you are not pure and can never be so." Elsewhere he said "The pain of the *javânmardân* is an anguish which the two worlds together could not contain."

TA 703, 4, 9

1. Cf. EE 69.
2. *Javânmardân* are those people who dedicate their being and everything they possess to their friend, or indeed anyone, expecting nothing in return.

Abu 'Othmân Ḥiri said, "The 'anguished one' is one who places too little importance on 'anguish' to be afraid of it."

TA 480

My sole preoccupation is anguish over you;
Night and day I'm constantly preoccupied with you.

'Aṭṭâr

When Râbe'a saw a man who continually exclaimed "Oh! Anguish!" she said to him, "Say instead 'Oh! Lack of anguish!' If you had anguish you would not dare cry about it."

RQ 209

LOVE'S ANGUISH *(anduh-e 'eshq)*

A disciple asked Shebli if he ever wept. He said, "Whatever occurs between our heart and our soul is hidden from the eye; whatever occurs outwardly is foreign to the path; the solution must be sought from within. My friend, anguish for God is pre-eternal but it does not come to everyone. At the moment when anguish casts its shadow on the lover's heart, the thunder-storm of a state resounds, the lightning of hope flashes, the rain of what is desired falls upon the plain of the heart and brings forth the variety of flowers therein: the narcissus of contentment, the flowering judas of satisfaction, the lily of trust in God, the jasmine of humility. Under the clouds of anguish, the lover busies himself, gathering the many-hued flowers of the garden of the heart and tying them into bouquets.

KAM X 40

WEAKNESS *(kalâl)*

Whenever God appears to the gnostic as Eternity *(qedam)*, Primacy *(awwaliyat)*, and Everlasting-ness *(sarmadiyat)*, the gnostic finds himself in the sea of the Uniqueness *(waḥdâniyat)* of pre-eternity *(azal)* and post-eternity *(abad)*, vanishing in the attributes of Splendour, Magnificence, Majesty and Might. The utmost awe and exaltation overcomes his heart and he loses the power of speech in the course of witnessing *(moshâhada)*. Even if he wished to describe God in the subtlest of expressions, the weakness of his tongue, caused by the onrush of descending lights of the Eternal and Subsistent, would not permit it.

The Prophet said, "When one comes to know God, one's tongue becomes weak and is incapable of speech."[1]

The gnostic said, "Sudden bewilderment at the moment of revelation of the Splendour causes the gnostic to become weak."

MA 155

You try your best, and finally, because of weakness
You tell yourself, "The intellect has hobbled me."

MM IV 3353

ENNUI *(malâl)*

'Ennui' refers to the torpor which arises from over-involvement in something, causing one to become fatigued and inertial, and thus, to turn away therefrom.

TJ 155

Whenever God's Might appears with all its attributes from the concealment of Eternity, He annihilates that which is other than Himself including the traditional states and stations of the path. The lights of His might envelop the spirit of the adherent to divine unity and he is overwhelmed by Sanctity. Because of the intensity of the theophany thereof, the wayfarer becomes agitated and seeks to be veiled from it, so that he might retain the pleasure of the infusions of God. This state may also occur at the station of intimacy. When the wayfarer has become perfected in intimacy, enjoying the vision of the nearness of the nearness *(qorb-e qorb)*, and remaining firm at the sight of intimacy through vision of beauty, he desires to be alone for a night, away from the intimacy of God. This occurs because of the powerlessness of the transitory in the face of the Eternal. The Prophet said, "I seek refuge in You from You," and "God does not accept ennui until you lack interest in yourself."

The gnostic said, "Ennui means the fleeing of the transitory from obliteration in Eternity."

MA 205

1. This saying is attributed to the 10th century Sufi master of Baghdad, Abo'l-Qâsem Jonaid by Hojwiri (KM, Nicholson's translation p. 356). It is not included in Wensinck's *Concordance of Muslim Traditions.*

The anguish of love for her
 is banned for those who fear Ennui;
It is either our head at her feet
 or our lips at her mouth.

Ḥâfeẓ

SORROW *(ḥozn)*

'Sorrow' signifies dispersion of the heart in the valleys of forgetfulness.

'Sorrow' is said to symbolise a condition which appears in the heart after dispersion has taken place and which causes 'seeking' with total effort and remorse for one's having fallen into dispersion.

EE 69

'Sorrow' signifies constriction of the heart.

SS 634

'Sorrow' is a type of happiness which is mixed with sadness. Sorrow is different from 'concern' *(hamm)*, in that 'concern' is a natural condition, whereas 'sorrow' is a condition which comes from God.

BT 734

From this book we make only one point:
 When there is sorrow within,
How can you make good poetry?

Ḥâfeẓ

'Sorrow' differs from sadness in that the former involves constriction of the heart, while the latter involves constriction of the breast.

According to the Koran, "...They turned back, their eyes streaming with tears of sorrow" (IX: 92).

'Sorrow' signifies suffering over what has been lost and remorse over what has not been gained, and it has three degrees. The first, 'sorrow of the ordinary people', stems from laziness in service, lapsing into impropriety and the wasting of one's days. The second, 'sorrow of the devotees', is caused by time spent in dispersion and the preoccupation of the *nafs* with contemplative vision. It is also caused by the calmness which preceeds sorrow. The elect however, do not linger in the station of sorrow. The third degree of 'sorrow' arises out of a preoccupation with worldly thoughts which are lower than gnostic perceptions, conflict between one's intentions, and conflict with that which has been decreed.

MS 46

'Sorrow' is one of the stations of the wayfarer which appears after the currents of attraction exerted by loving-kindness have merged in the care-worn heart. This occurs when continuous reflection and bewilderment overpower the mysteries of the wayfarer's inner conciousness and the pain which sets the inner consciousness alight concentrates the fire of yearning in all breaths. This is the quality for which Moḥammad is praised, when it is said that he was in continuous anguish and sorrow. The reality of sorrow is the burning of the worthy and capable nature by the fire created from the flint of the attributes of God, in the form of the lights of beauty and perfection, which strike that surrendered part of the rational spirit. The Prophet said, "God likes all sorrowful hearts."

MA 30

HUT OF SORROWS *(kolba-ye aḥzân)*

The 'hut of sorrows' is said to symbolise a time *(waqt)* of 'sorrow'.

EE 70

That Joseph who is missing will come back to Canaan;
    do not be sad!
The hut of sorrows will one day become a rose-garden;
    do not be sad!

Ḥâfeẓ

The 'hut of sorrows' symbolises the heart which is full of sadness because of separation from the Beloved.

KF 1561

The 'hut of sorrows' is said to symbolise the station of dispersion of the heart when 'sorrow' appears because of the loss of the True Sought One *(maṭlub-e ḥaqiqi).*

TT 223

Since I'll not find lost Joseph again in this world,
My breast must be a hut of sorrows.

'Erâqi

Where has he gone once more,
    making my heart a beggar's hut of sorrows,
That king who made the house
    of the heart a royal seat?

Kamâl Khojandi

ANXIETY *(ghoṣṣa)*

'Anxiety' is one of the stations of those who experience 'longing' *(eshtiyâq).* The 'anxiety' of the lover occurs when he falls into the sea of separation and the mist of the intensity of estrangement *(ferâq)* envelopes his heart. His spirit is then stirred to excitement by the fire of loving-kindness in his breast and the hot vapours of loving-kindness flow into his throat. As they build up, the lover tries unsuccessfully to swallow them, suffering an unpleasant burning. This continues until the host of the lights of serenity descends upon the lover's heart and the fragrant breezes of nearness waft therein. This causes him to complain in the form of crying and 'anxiety', whereupon he becomes unable to speak because of the overwhelming bitterness of estrangement and loss just after finding.

MA 111

He by whom each cypress is made free,
Has the power to turn anxiety into joy.

MM VI 1742

SIGH *(âh)*

The 'sigh' is said to symbolise intense regret on the part of the wayfarer over the wasting of his moments, as well as his complete readiness to make up for what has been lost.

The 'sigh' is said to symbolise the sign of the perfection of love which occurs at the level of spirit *(ṭaur-e ruḥi),*[1] which the tongue cannot adequately describe, its faculty of speech being unequal to the task of describing the reality thereof. As a consequence, out of anxiety and distress, a person will emit the sigh, 'Ah!', in order to relieve his anguish and dispel his grief, as God says, "Abraham was compassionate *(awwâh)* and clement" (IX: 114).

> When a sigh emerges from that special place,
> One experiences a state of liberation.

TT 173-174

> The sigh is tell-tale in the way of love and lover;
> Keep that sigh suppressed within the hidden chamber of silence.

Sanâ'i

SIGHING *(ta'awwoh)*

'Sighing' is the attribute of one who experiences a state in which his heart undergoes distress and anxiety while being full of loving-kindness and yearning. This state overcomes him because of the torments of loving-kindness which stem from prolonged estrangement and the fire of yearning. His breast tightens from the immensity of the intense assaults of God's magnificence. His heart dissolves from the relentless theophanies of Attributes. His spirit becomes annihilated by the searing that comes of the exaltation of viewing the Essence. Then he bursts out with such a sigh that breaths of gnosis and love ascend therefrom, as God describes his friend *Khalil* [Abraham], when He said, "Lo, Abraham was clement, compassionate *(awwâh)*, and penitent..." (XI: 75); that is to say, Abraham sighed in ecstasy from being overcome with yearning, this being one of the greatest signs of the gnostics.

The gnostic said, "Sighing comes from the freezing of the pens of the attributes upon the tablet of the spirit."

MA 111

1. See note on page 15.

LAMENTATION *(zâri)*

'Lamentation' is said to symbolise the heart's awakening to the realisation that true purpose has been lost in the past and that one has failed to achieve 'finding' *(wejdân)*[1] in the present.

> Wherever I go, the mosque or the winehouse,
> I find myself lamenting from your pain,
> Or crying 'Woe!' in yearning for you.

TT 201-202

> Every morning, a hundred times, I wail and lament
> For the zephyr to take a message from me to your lane.

'Erâqi

> You have no pain, nor a pallid face;
> O lover without pain,
> What are you lamenting and wailing about?

Kamâl Khojandi

WAILING *(nâla)*

'Wailing' is said to symbolise spiritual communion *(monâjât)*[2].

EE 70

'Wailing' is said to symbolise inward spiritual communion, which arises from the heart's complete attention to the essential origin, which is the true aim.

> Each morning the wailing of those bereft of heart
> Arises from pain of separation from her face.

TT 232

1. *See Sufi Symbolism,* Vol. I, p. 182.
2. Cf. KF 1563.

Let the bird who sings by night have good news
in the way of love;
The wails of those who remain awake at night
bring pleasure to the friend.

Ḥâfeẓ

From the winehouses arose the wailing of heartaches;
I do not know what constitutes the murmuring of love.

'Erâqi

Wailing in the pain of love is an affliction
that sears the breast.
How wretched is my feeble heart which constantly
bears affliction!

Kamâl Khojandi

KEENING *(nâla-ye zir)*[1]

'Keening' is said to represent the practice of the lover.

EE 66

I want a fine companion and a well-tuned bow-string
So that I may express my pain in keening and groaning.

Ḥâfeẓ

Wretched me! I am a captive of keening;
My beloved never asks, "How is this poor one?"

Rumi

MOANING *(nâla-ye zâr)*

'Moaning' is said to represent the lover's expression of gladness or sorrow.

EE 66

1. 'Keening' connotes a bitter wailing.

The morning wind told of the dust of her doorway;
A hundred moans arose from the ailing heart.

'Erâqi

Every night I moan in an indescribable way;
It's the wailing of separation
from the indescribable beloved.

Hâtef Eṣfahâni

GROAN *(anin)*

The 'groan' is said to represent the sound emitted by one in pain in response to the inflicter of the pain.

TJ 57

When the 'longing one' is trampled down by the realm of Divine Power *('âlam-e jabarut)*[1] and is injured by the wounds inflicted by the swords of theophany of the angelic realm *('âlam-e malakut)*[2], he groans, because of the breaths of nearness [to God], such a groan that sears the soul due to the burning of nearness and of closeness to God. This occurs while he burns in the fires of separation, estranged from his own inner consciousness in the wilderness of perpetuity and the deserts of pre-eternalness.

It is said that God likes the gnostic's 'groan'. A Tradition relates that when God hears the 'groan' of his friends, he boasts of it to the angels.

The gnostic said, "The groan of the yearning one is the call of the lover's spirit in the prison of loving-kindness."

MA 110

I am so drunk with love
that I have gone beyond all bounds;
As soon as I stopped my groaning,
that lovely one heard and came.

Rumi

1. See *Farhang-e Nurbakhsh,* Vol. 4, p.112.
2. Ibid p.108

Ḥâfeẓ have a thought for the beloved's sensitivity;
Leave her door and take your wails and groans away
with you.

Ḥâfeẓ

PLAINT or 'WOE!' *(feghân)*

The 'plaint' is said to symbolise the outer expression of the inner condition.

EE 70

O woe! That unkind lovely one, who loves to have
enemies:
How easily she disassociated herself from
her companions!

Ḥâfeẓ

The moon dissolved out of love for the night of your
tresses,
And the sun cried "Woe!" at the radiance of your
features.

Rumi

I am exhausted out of love for you;
Out of pain, my heart cries out, "O Woe!"

'Aṭṭâr

SCREAM *(waila)*

The 'scream' is said to represent the sign of the lover's perfection which the tongue cannot describe. It is the result of extreme compulsion, not of pretence.

EE 70

SHOUT *(shahqa)*

The 'shout' refers to God's call in the world, which summons the soaring spirits of the realm of existence to the sources of nearness.

SS 633

In most cases the 'shout' is the result of the wayfarer's attempt to comprehend divine utterance *(kheṭâb)* at stations of presence and contemplative vision.

When, in the course of the contemplation of lights the wayfarer hears the subtleties of God's utterance in his heart, he comes to taste the sweetness of the mysteries of utterance, and, experiencing pleasure in the purity of God's words, his spirit becomes unable to withstand the onslaught of that utterance. At this point, if he does not comprehend the utterance, but only hears it, or if he understands and perceives the meaning of the utterance according to his level of nearness to God, he will shout.

By the same token, the comprehension of any divine utterance on the part of the sincere hearer may lead to shouts and cries accompanied by either reverence and exaltation, nearness or union, fear and awe, or rebuke and punishment.

However, the wayfarer may also experience states arising from the viewing of the brilliance of the attributes and beauty of the Essence, unaccompanied by utterance. One sort of state comes in vision of the acquisition, or appearance of attributes or acts, or the manifestation of the Essence. For each of the wayfarer's states there is a different level of ecstasy which varies with the wayfarer's changing condition, expressed, for example, in the form of 'shouting', 'shrieking', the rending of garments and so forth, there being so many forms that we cannot name them all; the 'shout' serves as a key example of one of the reactions of the 'finders' *(ahl-e wojud)*.

Have you not heard how the Prophet shouted when he heard Ebn Mas'ud recite the verse, "And how will it be when We bring forward a witness from every community, and We bring you [Moḥammad] forward as a witness against these?" (Koran IV: 41).

A gnostic said, "Whenever the sincere gnostic shouts for the sake of God, he encompasses east and west."

The gnostic said, "Whenever the lover begins to shout, his heart dissolves in his beloved."

MA 92

CRYING *(gerya)*[1]

The Sufi's 'crying' may arise from burning by the fire of need *(niyâz)*, within which the traces of *nafs* are hidden. 'Crying' may also arise from the fire of yearning *(shauq)*, in which case it is expressed in laughter.

1. *Al-bakâ'.*

'Crying' in love is one of the forms of the selfishness of the *nafs*. 'Crying' in seclusion is for the sake of solace; in the company of others, it is an expression of inner conflagration; both cases involve selfishness of the *nafs*, for the lover 'cries' only when he is conscious of himself.

LA 57

Blind be the eye that is not disgraced by love's crying;
Dark is the heart which lacks the light of loving-kindness.

Ḥâfeẓ

'Crying' arises from regrets; regret arises from the loss of the Beloved, as when the master of Canaan [Jacob] cried so much that the pupil of his eye, which was the vicegerent of the visible realm, lost its outward form and became white, blinded by grief. However, the travellers on this Way experience no regret or sorrow, because they do not fear the loss of the Beloved...

The cause of 'crying' in the lover's eye is the jealousy *(ghairat)* which the reality of the lover's being has for God. This reality of his being, of which love is the attribute, wishes, because of jealousy, to see the eye of the lover become blind and lose hope in seeing, for it knows that this physical eye hinders true beholding.

Tears of blood flow from my eyes,
For they are not worthy of seeing you.

It is permissable, therefore, that one cries so much that one becomes dazzled and does not look upon the beauty of that charmer for fear that her delicate face would be wounded by one's look, as in the verse:

I cannot look sharply at her face,
For fear that she'd be wounded
in her delicateness.

LA 58

When Abu Sa'id Kharrâz was asked about 'crying', he said, "Crying is from God, about God, and for God."

'Crying from God' arises from the duration of His torment. One also cries in remembering the length of time that passes before one beholds Him. 'Crying' may also arise from fear of separation, and out of fear of what God has promised for those who have been heedless of his commands. Agitation also causes crying when one is fearful that certain things might happen which could prevent one from reaching God.

'Crying about God' may mean that one's inner consciousness displays excitement towards God. 'Crying' may come from the flights of spirits in yearning towards of God; or it may be from the fascination of the intellect with God; or again, it may be from regret, or in standing before God, or out of sensitivity while one is complaining to God. 'Crying' may also occur when one rubs one head in the dust while begging God for closeness to Him. It may also arise from the pressure of competition with others, whenever one imagines that union with Him has been delayed or that one might fall behind and never reach God, or out of fear that one is unworthy of beholding God, or out of shame that one lacks the eyes to see him with.

'Crying for God' may mean that God has delayed his attention to one when one has become accustomed to expecting his attention. It may also come from joy in union with God, where one is enveloped in God's mercy, like a suckling baby crying as it suckles at its mother's breast.

LT 229

'Crying' is one of the stations of the 'longing ones' *(moshtâqân)*.

The characteristic that most distinguishes the longing ones is 'crying', which represents the connection of the heart of the longing one with the beauty of the Beloved. This is caused by the effect of the heat of the spirit generated by the lights of theophany. Furthermore, it marks every station in gnosis. 'Crying' obtains in proportion to the degree of the revelation of the attributes; since revelations of the attributes are infinite, so the crying of the 'longing ones' is infinite. Many of the longing ones have cried when viewing the Magnificence, or the Beauty or the Majesty, or upon the viewing the Eternal or the Subsistent, or when hearing divine utterance, or upon the unveiling of direct vision of the seas of the Essence. The number of such stations is countless, for they are revelations of pre-eternity, the gifts of Divine Everlastingness *(sarmadiyat)*, and only those who experience yearning and gnosis recognise them.

In the words of the Koran, "And when they hear what has been revealed to the Prophet, you see their eyes flow with tears from their recognising the truth"(V: 83).

In one of his prayers, the Prophet petitioned, "O Lord, provide that my eyes ever pour with tears in fear of you."[1]

The Prophet maintained that the truths of 'crying' are located at the site of knowledge of God; this is why it is the noblest level amongst all stations, and why this 'crying' is the sublimest kind of crying, because the one who is 'crying' is engaged in viewing the Magnificence, the Splendour, and the Majesty; and in the sweet perception of these attributes no trace of human consciousness can be found. Those birds flying towards these stations fly with wings of yearning and 'crying'.

The gnostic said, "The 'crying' of the longing one, realised in yearning comes from God, is about God and for God."

Sarrâj said, "Crying is the flight of spirits towards God by way of lamentation."

MA 110

CRYING FROM GOD TO GOD
(geristan az ḥaqq bar ḥaqq)[2]

Whenever the crescent moon of the Beauty becomes hidden from the sight of the gnostic, he cries from God to God, due to the loss of Majesty.

The gnostic said, "Crying from God to God arises from extreme yearning for him.

MA 265

CRYING IN LAUGHTER *(geristan dar khanda)*[3]

When intimacy with God's Beauty overcomes God's vicegerent *(khalifa)* in the course of his viewing that Beauty, and God appears to him in a guise appropriate to intimacy, exhilaration overcomes him. As his spirit recognises God, tears flow from his eyes; as his spirit laughs, he sees his spirit's laughter in his face. Thus, while breaking out in laughter, he cries with exhilaration and gladness in God.

The gnostic said, "Laughing and crying in ecstasy arise from God's concern for his lover at the station of intimacy."

MA 280

1. Cited in Foruzânfar, *Aḥâdith-e Mathnawi* (Tehran: 1981) No. 666.
2. *Al-bakâ' men al-ḥaqq alâ al-ḥaqq.*
3. *Al-bakâ' fe'ḍh-dhaḥk.*

CRYING IN ECSTASY *(geristan dar wajd)*[1]

This state has different levels due to the surge of affectionate attachment on the part of the spirit; which draws tears from the eye during contemplative vision of the Divine Beauty in the form of gnosis of the revelation of the lights of the attributes and the illumination of the Essence.

The gnostic said, "Crying occurs in more than a thousand stations, the most distinctive and noblest being that of gnosis."

MA 285

ACQUAINTANCESHIP *(âshnâ'i)*

'Acquaintanceship' signifies the attachment of the subtlety *(daqiqa)* of Lordship to all creatures, like that of the Creator to the creation.

KF 1551[2]

'Acquaintanceship' is said to symbolise the attachment of the primal favour and the relationship of pre-eternal mercy to all existent things.

Since your heart is alien, whatever I tell you
About acquaintanceship will seem to be only a
fairy tale.

TT 170-171

After all, my heart has enjoyed acquaintanceship with
you till now;
Has an acquaintance ever done to an acquaintance
what you have done to me?

'Erâqi

Don't be a stranger, for 'Aṭṭâr has
Come to you in acquaintanceship.

'Aṭṭâr

1. *Al-bakâ 'fe'l-wajd.*
2. Cf. EE 57.

To the ones who have illuminated eyes, I give
A greeting like the fragrance of acquaintanceship.

Ḥâfeẓ

ALIENATION AND THE STRANGER
(bigâna wa bigânagi)

'Alienation' is said to represent the self-sufficiency of the realm of Divinity *(oluhiyat)*, which is completely free of need for anything and absolutely incomparable with anything.

RA 51

What alternative has the lover except to be driven mad?
What's the beloved's coyness for except to alienate?

Rumi

O friend, come forth, for I am yours;
Don't play the stranger, for we are acquainted.

'Erâqi

'Alienation' is said to symbolise the self-sufficiency of the realm of Divinity,[1] which shines upon the core of the heart of the wayfarer, so that, just as the self-sufficient Essence of the Absolute is free of all need, it alienates the lover from all other things, including self and kin.

The thought of your face drives us to madness,
Alienating us from self and all acquaintances.

TT 180

When the fish seeks acquaintance in the sea,
He becomes alienated from all fish.

'Aṭṭâr

1. *'Âlam Lahut,* see *Farhang-e Nurbakhsh,* Vol. 4, p. 116.

When you became acquainted with the sea,
you were alienated from self;
When those tresses came into your hand,
you were delivered from distress.

'Erâqi

An acolyte, who was a brigand of religion, passed by;
My heart, following that acquaintance became a stranger
to all.

Ḥâfeẓ

The 'alien' or 'stranger' *(bigâna)* is one who has fallen behind on the path.

LG II 7

RESPONSE *(ejâbat)*

'Response' represents the granting of the appeal of a petitioner who enjoys closeness to God.

SS 635

The map of Tabriz[1] was imagined in my heart,
For it is the *qebla*[2] of response, and the heart is God's
house.

Rumi

When I drop down by your visage, I need a kiss;
The morning prayer of hope requires response.

Kamâl Khojandi

BANISHMENT *(ṭard)*

'Banishment' is rare and occurs when a gnostic close to God attains the station of the nearness *(qorb-e qorb)* and is close to being consumed and annihilated in the magnificence of God because of the fullness of his yearning for annihilation in God. At this point, God

1. The city in north western Iran from which Shams, Rumi's master, came.
2. The direction in which Moslems pray.

banishes the gnostic from Himself and from nearness to Him, so that he may not be consumed and annihilated.

This 'banishment' is without anger; rather, it expresses God's intention to test and purify the gnostic and increase his sincerity in adherence to the divine unity; it also leads to his becoming one with God, through perceiving that which is the reatest veil before union. This is why the Prophet said, "The sincere ones are in a great danger."

The gnostic said, "Banishment is the jealousy *(ghairat)* of the Eternal, so that there will be nothing but the Eternal with the Eternal."

MA 190

HELP *(yâri)*

'Help' symbolises the aid bestowed by pre-eternal favour, which brings about the wayfarer's attainment of high degrees and sublime stations.

TT 237

You who have no interest in helping me, why do you
Come into my dreams in the middle of every night?

Bâbâ Ṭâher

Come, companion, and help my heart,
For a poor wretch has no companion but you.

'Erâqi

TRIBULATION *(meḥnat)*

'Tribulation' is said to represent the trouble and pain inflicted on the lover by the Beloved, whether willingly suffered or imposed.

There is no point in explaining my tribulation:
Just look at my flowing tears; there lies the explanation.

EE 70[1]

1. Cf. TT 227.

O you blood-thirsty heart, look for your own
tribulation,
For that companion has lost interest in association
with us.

'Erâqi

Since I cannot bear the sadness
of tribulation and alienation,
I will go back to my own town
and there be my own ruler.

Ḥâfeẓ

You told me you would kill me with tribulation;
As far as I am concerned nothing better
could happen to me!

Kamâl Khojandi

'Tribulation' and 'affliction' *(balâ')* are trials for the heart and soul. They are characteristics of 'loving-kindness' and bring to light the perfections and imperfections of the wayfarer. The Beloved sets the trap of affliction, while scattering the seeds of bestowal. The boon of loving-kindness is blended with divine bestowal and affliction.

Loving-kindness is the pearl and affliction the oyster. The oyster is the excuse while the pearl is that which is bestowed. Loving-kindness is the rose and fidelity its thorn. What seeker has not suffered? For whoever fancies the rose is not bothered by the pricks of a thorn. Slaying the lover is the custom of this court, and indifference the attitude of this monarch. 'Tribulation' and loving-kindness go hand-in-hand, they are old friends. The alchemy of loving-kindness does not come free; affliction comes cheap for the soul of the lover. You must have a thousand souls to spend on the Friend in your passion for Him. 'Affliction' with friendship is fine, even though it is all fire.

RJ 124

EASE *(râḥat)*

'Ease' is said to symbolise liberation of the heart from enslavement to the *nafs* and its passions.

If you seek ease, be a companion in his pain;
If you seek luck, be a companion in love with him.

TT 199

'Ease' is said to represent something that accords with the heart's will.

EE 71

Where are you, O ease of my heart?
Where are you, who has made my soul love-crazed?

Rumi

Though sadness for you diminishes my soul,
Recollection of your face delightfully increases ease.

'Erâqi

Sâqi, pass the wine around, ease my soul,
For the circling heavens oppress my mind.

Ḥâfeẓ

You're a treasure
which without seeking cannot be found;
Without suffering,
ease from you cannot be found.

Kamâl Khojandi

Expressions like 'ease of spirit' *(râḥat-ruḥ)*, 'ease of heart' *(râḥat-del)* and 'ease of soul' *(râḥat-jân)* are allusions to the theophany of the Essence, representing states in which the wayfarer forgets everything other than God.

Ease of spirit and peace of heart arrived,
Illumination for my bloodshot eyes.
Gesturing amourously it came and
settled in my heart;
Shams became a stranger for me at that moment.

Rumi

ABJECT ONE *(dhalil)*

The 'abject one' symbolises the devotee enslaved by, and the wayfarer entangled in, the seductions of the commanding self *(nafs-e ammâra).*

TT 199

Even though you may resemble a lion, you'll turn
out like a fox, astray and abject,
If you proceed on this path without a guide.

MM IV 543

I'm exalted by your majesty, made abject by your
humbling,
For I am of Abraham's progeny, tempered by this
fire [of love].

Rumi

GRIEVED *(ḥasrân)*

To be 'grieved' is said to symbolise a contracted state in the heart[1] arising from the departure of the Beloved, which in turn stimulates the utmost earnestness of effort toward regaining the Sought One.

TT 192-93

VEXATION, 'ALAS!' *(afsus)*

'Vexation' is said to symbolise the regret of the wayfarer over his lost moments and the resolve to make up for that which has been missed.

TT 171

The heart has sought and failed to find you — Alas!
It's stymied now on how to seek you out.

'Erâqi

1. *Qabz,* for further discussion of this subject see the authors, *Sufism: Fear & Hope,* (New York: 1982).

Alas! She left, and in my crying eye
The trace of her image is washed away.

Ḥâfeẓ

Is it right that from one so generous as you
My share should be subjection to vexation?

Rumi

DESTITUTION *(bi-nawâ'i)*

'Destitution' is said to represent powerlessness.

EE 71

'Destitution' is said to symbolise the heart's distance and deprivation from the True Sought One *(maṭlub-e ḥaqiqi)* because of the obstacles of human nature.

Whoever becomes separated from one
  who speaks his language, is destitute,
Although he may possess a hundred fortunes.[1]

TT 180

'Destitution' is said to symbolise the detachment from both outward action and inward states and not being inclined to either.

RA 86

ABASEMENT *(oftâdagi)*

'Abasement' represents the manifestation of divine states accompanied by the awareness of one's powerlessness in practising servanthood that is worthy of God.

EE 71

When you are abased, 'Erâqi, do not turn your face
Away, if you wish to see the beloved's face.

'Erâqi

1. MM I 28.

We have stumbled and become abased;
give a hand to those who have fallen!
Eager for the chalice of wine,
we have fallen in anxiety.

Shâh Ne'mato'llâh

PALLID FACE *(zard-ru'i)*[1]

The 'pallid face' is said to symbolise the quality of conduct on the Path.

If you'd place your ruddy complexion
next to my pallid face;
What a lovely rose we'd make,
truly what a lovely rose!

TT 202

I am not two-faced[2] with you,
except, that is,
Where my black fortune mixes with
my pallid face.

Kamâl Khojandi

SHAMEFACEDNESS *(siyah-ru'i)*[3]

'Shamefacedness' is said to symbolise the attribute of need on the part of contingent being, as is illustrated in the following verse of Shabestari:

In both worlds shamefacedness
Will always be a trait inherent
in contingent being.

TT 208

1. The 'pallid face' represents the suffering and anxiety experienced on the Path.
2. In Persian this is rendered as 'two-coloured', which has the implicit meaning of 'two faced'.
3. Literally 'black-faced'.

FAMILIARITY *(olfat)*

In Sufi terminology, 'familiarity' is one of the levels of 'loving kindness', representing the inclination of the heart towards the object of familiarity *(ma'luf)*.

It is said that 'familiarity' has five degrees, the first being 'consciousness of the Acts of the Creator'. At this degree, 'friendship' is quickened in one's heart for a beautiful person simply by hearing mention of certain attributes of that person through a third party.

The second degree is 'concealment of the heart's inclination and tolerance of hardship'. Here the 'familiar one' *(alif)* seeks to hide his state, though his pallid face and moist eyes may give him away.

The third degree is that of 'wish' *(tamannâ)* where there is no thought of life or death. Although attainment of this station is difficult or even impossible, it is said that it is sweet to die with this desire.

The fourth degree is the giving and seeking of news on the part of the 'familiar one'. Here the 'familiar one' seeks to give news of himself and to receive news about the object of his 'familiarity' in return. Sometimes, maddened in desperation, he seeks to tell his secret to the zephyr *(ṣabâ)*; and sometimes he seeks a response from the breeze *(nasim)*.[1]

The fifth degree is that of 'beseeching', where the 'familiar one' engages in supplication and lamentation.

KF 79

Since I am not familiar with created beings,
People tend to think that I am mad.

Rumi

JOY *(sorur)*

'Joy'[2] is said to represent the gladness of a heart in which God's light and constant delight *('aish)*[3] are found.

Shams of Tabriz, remove the mask of Magnificence;
Bring joy to the souls who yearn for the candle of your face.

Rumi

1. See *Farhang-e Nurbakhsh*, Vol. IV, p.34, 35.
2. See *Sufi Symbolism,* Vol. I, p. 178.
3. *Ibid,* p. 179.

Whenever the attracted spirit falls in love with the bride of theophany and enters the garden of sanctity, it becomes 'joyful' through the knowledge of being accepted and selected by God. Whenever the lights of Beauty are revealed to it, it becomes joyful from God to God by God.

The Koran says, "They rejoice because of bounty from God" (III: 171).

The gnostic said, "The gnostic's joy is from the continuous awareness of perpetuity."

MA 88

The ninety-fourth field is that of joy, which arises from the field of visionary disclosure *(mokâshafa).*

"Say, 'In God's bounty and in His mercy let them rejoice; it is better than that which they hoard" (X: 58).

Joy is of three kinds, the first being 'joy in that which is prohibited' *(ḥarâm)*, the second, 'joy in that which is discouraged' *(makruh)*, and the third, 'joy in that which is obligatory' *(wâjeb).*

The 'prohibited joy' is joy in sinning, as indicated in God's words, "Exult not, Lo! God loves not the exultant" (XXVIII: 76) and "He is exultant, boastful" (XI: 10).

The 'discouraged joy' is where one is made joyous by the world, as alluded to in the verses, "And they rejoice in the life of the world" (XIII: 26), and "Do not rejoice in what has been bestowed upon you" (LVII: 23).

The 'obligatory joy' is joy in God, as referred to in the verse, "Then, rejoice in the transaction which you have concluded [with God]" (IX: 111).

'Joy in the prohibited' causes the heart to die, saps one's endurance, and turns friend into foe.

'Joy in that which is discouraged' detracts from one's self respect, increases turmoil, and requires that one give one's life in return.

'Joy in what is obligatory' is of three kinds, the joy in being a Moslem, which removes fetters, opens doors, and grants admittance to God; the joy of obligation to God, which frees one from reproach, liberates one from heaven, and gladdens one with Reality; and friendship [with God] which provides one direct intimacy [with God], wealth without riches, and might without armies.

SM 339

"Say, 'In God's bounty and in His mercy, therein let them rejoice; it is better than that which they accumulate" (X: 58).

'Joy' means receiving good tidings in the fullest of senses. It is purer than 'elation' *(faraḥ)* for 'elation' may be mixed with sorrow *(ḥozn)*. Accordingly, the Koran uses the word *faraḥ* in several places when referring to the world, whereas *sorur* is mentioned twice with respect to the hereafter.

In this context, 'joy' is of three degrees. The first, the 'joy of tasting' *(dhauq)*, removes three sorrows: the sorrow arising from fear of severance from the Prophetic heritage, the sorrow which is provoked by the darkness of ignorance, and the sorrow which arises from fear of dispersion.

The second, the 'joy of witnessing' *(moshâhada)*, removes the veil covering [Divine] knowledge, breaks the bonds of dogmatic ritual, and negates the remnants of self-will.

The third, the 'joy of hearing [God's] response *(ejâbat)*', obliterates any fear of distance [from God], brings contemplative vision *(moshâhada)*, and laughter to the spirit.

MS 176

DELIGHT, REJOICING *(neshaṭ)*

At the time when the terrestial and celestial natures of the lover are conjoined into an homogenous whole, the supersensible light of the vision of mystical illumination is cast upon the surface of the mind's mirror; God grants the spirit understanding of its divine reception through certain symptoms which overcome it and by [its audition of] the divine summons and the flinging wide of the gates of the divine mysteries and lights. The spirit then contemplates the hidden subtleties of the manifestation of the divine qualities insofar as they abide in hope and certainty. The more this marvelous station is apprehended, the more the spirit soars aloft on the wings of yearning *(shauq)* and love, rejoicing in its familiarity with the invisible. All of this, though is but a breath wafted from the station of yearning.

The gnostic said, "The 'delight' of the sincere arises from their realisation of the grace involved in God's apprehension of them, throughout all trials and tribulations which beset them, and their awareness of the Subsistence of the Eternal Being *(baqâ'o'l-qadim)*, inasmuch as time is absent from God's everlasting nature. Hence, there develops within them a subsistence in God *(ḥaqq)* free of abatement or weariness.

MA 84-85

Fervour for the beloved has been my religion for some
time;
The sorrow in this is delight for my sad heart.

Ḥâfeẓ

LAUGHTER, LAUGHING *(khanda, khandidan, ḍhaḥk)*

For the visionaries of the Eternal, the vision of 'laughter' in God's attributes is the manifestation of the highest heaven through the Beauty of the Eternal, in a humanly perceptible form. This experience, however, is a deception.

SS 64

Where with a glance she sends a dart into my heart,
She nourishes the soul of Ḥâfeẓ with a covert laugh.

Ḥâfeẓ

FELICITY *(sa'âdat)*

'Felicity' is said to represent the pre-eternal call from God.[1]

EE 71

Show me the way out of the darkness of consternation
Through the grace of the chalice illumined with your
felicity.

Ḥâfeẓ

Happy tidings, lovers! Because of our felicity such
a guest has now arrived.
The life of lives, the relishing of relishings,
the soul of souls!

Rumi

1. Cf. KF 640.

In the annals of his felicity,
 the one who suffers pain in love
Cannot gain successful mention
 without the pangs of tribulation.

Kamâl Khojandi

ALCHEMY OF FELICITY *(kimiyâ-ye sa'âdat)*

The 'alchemy of felicity' is said to represent the company of a good companion and the avoidance of a bad companion.

Alas! Till now I did not know
That the alchemy of felicity means a
 'good companion'!

Ḥâfeẓ

Let me teach you the alchemy of felicity:
Keep away from bad companionship.

Ḥâfeẓ

The 'alchemy of felicity' represents the refinement of the self through the avoidance of vice and purgation of its base qualities, as well as the acquisition of virtues with which to adorn the self.

ES 70

ELATION *(faraḥ)*

'Elation' is said to represent expansion of the heart through the influx *(tawârod)* of sacred grace *(faiḍh-e qodsi)* and infusions *(wâred)*,[1] once the outward faculties have been closed off through intimate association with God. This is illustrated in Ḥâfeẓ's verse:

Now that a breeze of paradise
 is wafting from the scented garden,
I have an elating wine
 and a heavenly companion.

TT 220

1. See *Spiritual Poverty in Sufism*, London: 1984, p. 65-80.

'Elation' signifies the casting off the heaviness of worldly existence from the site of vision of the inner consciousness *(serr).*

SS 635

'Elation' is one of the stations of the lovers.

The basis of this station is the vision *(ro'yat)* of God's beauty, and of knowledge of God's subsistence and perpetuity, as well as the hearing of the subtleties of God's utterance in the chambers of intimacy through the light of sanctity, where the blessings and bounties of God become manifest. As the visionary revelation of Beauty is increased for the lover, his intimacy with God increases, and when intimacy is increased 'elation' increases accordingly.

The Koran says, "Let them be elated therein..." (X: 59); and all these [that which is encompassed by God's bounty and mercy] are amongst the fruits of loving-kindness. Hence, 'elation' is one of the qualities of the lover, and arises from the dictates of loving-kindness, the site of divine unity *(tauḥid)*, and the gnosis of the antiquity of God's beneficence and the precedence of His mercy before His wrath in favour of His sincere lovers. How may 'elation' not be found by one to whom God appears in the guise of beauty, which forever stimulates the hearts of lovers by way of 'elation' and 'joy'?

The gnostic said, "Elation means gladness of spirit in the subtleties of divine emanations."

MA 94

I am elated, for like a bud,
I have drunk this chalice of wine,
while hiding my heart under my collar.

'Aṭṭâr

The more you drink the heart's blood,
the more elated you become,
And if you want to take my soul,
you do so with rapture.

Sa'di

ELATION IN ABSENCE *(faraḥ dar ghaibat)*

'Elation in absence' is one of the stations of the recipients of mysteries, who are among the Noble Ones *(nojabâ')*. This 'elation' is the yearning of the spirit for God and involves the remembrance of the moments of union. Through this elation, the tether of veiling is untied from the foot of the bird of the spirit, so that it may take flight on the wings of 'elation' to the realm of rejoicing *(shâdmâni)*.

Ḥallâj said, "Elation towards God brings about increase in exhilaration in the witnessing *(moshâhada)* of God."

MA 265

KINDNESS *(mehrbâni)*

'Kindness' is an attribute of Lordship *(robubiyat)*[1]

EE 58

'Kindness' is said to be an atribute of Lordship, which arises from the fullness of favour and kindness brought to bear in the training and development of the wayfarer.

TT 230

Once we turn our faces
    from this shameless world,
We shall gaze upon the face
    of that kind one.

'Erâqi

SOUL-QUICKENING *(jân-afzâ'i)*

'Soul-quickening' is said to represent the attribute of post-eternal subsistence which is not subject to annihilation.

EE 58

They will pass from darkness
    to the wellspring of the water of life,
And at every moment with heart and soul,
    drink from that soul-quickening chalice.

'Erâqi

1. Cf. KF 1563.

Subsistence in God was not due to my soul, but to love,
For what I have discovered is that soul-quickening love.

'Aṭṭâr

From the Sufi point of view, 'soul-quickening' is said to refer to the subsistence through which the wayfarer becomes post-eternally subsistent and is not subject to annihilation.

KF 1555

'Soul-quickening' is said to symbolise the attribute of subsistence, which is obtained through the subsistence of the Beauty of God, by the wayfarer once the traces of human nature are annihilated from him. Through this attribute, he becomes post-eternally subsistent and everlastingly existent; this condition is no longer subject to annihilation, "...In killing him, We are the blood money."[1] As illustrated by Shabestari:

Hidden behind the veil of every particle
is the soul-quickening beauty
Of the face of the soul-of-souls.

TT 186

HEART-OPENING *(del-goshâ'i)*

'Heart-opening' is said to represent the attribute of the opener of the heart at the station of intimacy.

EE 58

Grant clarity to the mirror of my heart with your regard,
That I might see within in your heart-opening radiant face.

'Erâqi

1. Sacred Tradition. See the author's *In the Tavern of Ruin,* p. 23-24.

The moment that God drew the line
of your heart-opening eyebrow,
The solution to my problem became subject
to your flirtation.

Ḥâfeẓ

'Heart-opening' is said to symbolise the station of concentration *(jam'iyat),* which is the fullest expanse of the heart, encompassing all the levels of theophany in such a way that unity does not veil multiplicity nor multiplicity veil unity. As Shabestari writes:

The concentration of the concentration
is the station of his heart-opening;
His soul-quickening beauty is
the candle of concentration.

TT 197

I am happy in my heart without a heart-opener;
I am suffering but I have no consoler.

'Aṭṭâr

EXCITEMENT *(hayajân)*

'Excitement' symbolises the fervour of the inner consciousness for the light of the realm of the unseen.

SS 633

The sincere lover is constantly enmeshed in the web of God's attraction. With the revelation of the mystery of the unseen within his inner consciousness and through that which his spirit sees, his inner consciousness is stirred to 'excitement'. When the disciple begins witnessing, in yearning for more, the seas of his excitement are whipped into waves.

'Excitement' characterises lovers when they are attracted *(majdhub).* When they attain union, their excitement abates.

The gnostic said, "Excitement refers to the flaring up of the fires of loving-kindness after the revelation of the Beauty of the Beloved".

MA 88

In Sufi terminology 'taste' signifies the drunkenness which the lover experiences in the 'tasting' of the wine of love. It also signifies the yearning which occurs with audition *(samâ')* of the Beloved's words, and in the witnessing and beholding of Him, which brings the lover into ecstasy, rendering him selfless such that he becomes obliterated in the Absolute.

The heart which lacks the fire of yearning
Does not know the sweetness of tasting.

Sanâ'i

When, through tasting, I saw the wine,
the Sâqi and the goblet as one,
I appealed to people to forget Islam and unbelief.

'Aṭṭâr

'Taste' is said to symbolise a mystical light which God, through his theophany, shines in the hearts of His friends, so that they may distinguish between truth and falsehood without referring to books or other secondary sources.

TJ 73

What is tasting? It is to become
aware of spiritual reality,
Though not through piety
or a cleric's decree.

'Aṭṭâr

What is tasting? Sampling the dew of promise,
Then craving the magnificent ocean.

MN 41

The tasting of people only increases
weakness in the body;
That taste from God
increases heart and soul, dear soul.

Rumi

'Tasting' is the first of the degrees of the vision of God through God; it occurs during rapidly successive flashes *(bawâreq)*, lasting longer than the lightning *(barq)* of theophany. If it continues, and approaches the mid-point of the station of vision, it is called 'drinking' *(shorb)*; and if its duration reaches the limit, it is referred to as 'quenching' *(rayy)*. These degrees vary according to the purity of the inner consciousness in not seeing that which is other than God.[1]

ES 162

'Taste' is the first degree of vision and manifestation of God to the wayfarer in a state of the sparkling flashes of loving-kindness. This vision varies in level according to the capacity of the witness and his aptitude for 'tasting' and 'drinking'. The purer his capacity for 'tasting' is from adulteration with the bitterness of corrupt humours, the more the perception of the witnessed will increase the purity of the sweetness of union and of vision.

The gnostic knows, while one who has not tasted cannot know.

TT 199

In the early stages 'tasting' takes the form of consciousness of grace which has been given in the form of nourishment, maintenance, and responsibility. In the final stages it takes the form of the vision of God through God in the reality of concentration *('ain-e jam')*.

RSh IV 180

'Tasting' is the initial stage of 'drinking'. Its reality is the heart's discovery, through union, of the sweetness of the purity of purities.

SS 627

'Tasting' is similar to 'drinking' *(shorb)* except that 'drinking' refers only to pleasure, while 'tasting' may apply to pleasure and pain alike. For example, one might say, 'I tasted opposition', or 'I tasted ease', or 'I tasted affliction', whereas when referring to 'drinking', one would only say, 'I drank the cup of union and love'. There are numerous examples concerning this, as in the Koran, "Eat and drink to your heart's content"(LXXVII: 43), while on the subject of 'tasting' it says, "Taste thou this; truly wast thou mighty, full of

1. Cf. KF 153.

honour"[1] (XLIV: 49), and elsewhere, "Taste ye the touch of hell..." (LIV: 48).

KM 508

The first station experienced by lovers is the tasting from goblets filled with the oceans of mystical illumination *(tajalli)*. As they contemplate the radiance of divine intimacy in their hearts, redolent with fragant breezes wafted from the invisible realm, the wide plains of the illumination of divine qualities are revealed to them. As the most mysterious aspect of their spirits inclines towards intimacy with God, they realise the purity of 'heart-savour' and experience the radiance of unveiled contemplative vision.

Dho'n-Nun said, "When God wants to make his friends drink from the chalice of his loving-kindness, he fills them with his pleasures, causing them to taste the sweetness thereof.

The gnostic said, "Tasting is the life of disciples, wherein lies the relishing of those who keep the night vigil."

MA 117

'Tasting' lasts longer than ecstasy and possesses greater illumination than 'lightning' *(barq)*. It has three degrees:

The first is the 'attestation to the tasting of divine promise', which the intellect cannot perceive, and which cannot be cut off by worldly expectations, or impeded by complacency.

The second degree is the 'desire to taste intimacy' in such a way that no other occupation becomes involved with it, no obstacle disturbs it, and no distraction vitiates it.

The third degree is tasting severance with the flavour of unification, tasting aspiration with the flavour of concentrated consciousness and tasting the nightly spiritual communion *(mosâmara)* with the flavour of contemplative vision.

MS 166

PLEASURE *(ledhdhat)*

In Sufi terminology 'pleasure' is said to represent that agreeable feeling which comes through witnessing the beauty of the Beloved.

1. This verse was revealed to the Prophet after Abu Jahl, one of his enemies, said to him, "You can do no harm to me because I am mighty and noble." Cf. KAM IX, 113-114.

You are the peerless giver of spirit;
You are the pleasure of knowledge and action.
All the rest is pretext and fraud:
To say "This is the sickness" and "That is the cure!"

Rumi

O you who are not aware of the endless pleasure
of our drinking,
We have seen the reflection of the beloved's face
in the light filled beaker.

Ḥâfeẓ

When the love drinks up the wine of nearness from the chalice of exhilaration, he experiences 'pleasure'. Once he tastes the sweetness of that wine in his inner being, the higher level of 'tasting' is attained and this is the inward journey of the light of contemplative vision within the source of the inner consciousness. Have you not read the words of the Prophet, where he asks God, "I beg of You the pleasure of gazing upon Your beneficent aspect." Thus, he had come to realise that 'pleasure' comes hand in hand with the revelation of witnessing: it is more complete than 'tasting'.

Ḥallâj said, "Pleasure is the experiencing of the taste of union in the viewing of the Beauty."

MA 117

RELISH *(ṭa'm)*

When the lover seated at the festive spread of mutual intimacy *(mo'ânesat)* becomes sated with the banquet of contemplative vision, and relishes the fruits of the trees of witnessing and comprehends the truths of union, his state stems from the source of 'seeing' directly, not indirectly by way of account or effect. This state is that of 'relish' and is more powerful than 'pleasure'.

The gnostic said, "To attain witnessing under the condition of expansion is referred to as 'relishing'."

MA 117

DRINKING *(shorb)*

In Sufi terminology this term refers to the sweetness of worship *(tâ'at)*, coupled with the pleasure of divine grace and the ease of intimacy. No progress can be made without it. Just as the body drinks water, so the heart drinks the ease and sweetness of the heart. Hojwiri's master said that the disciple and the gnostic must not be strangers to drinking, devotion and gnosis. Someone else has said that the disciple must 'drink' through his own actions in order to seek God with devotion, while the gnostic must not 'drink' because he may attain ease not through God, but by 'drinking', and hence rest in his *nafs.*

KM 507

'Drinking' for the pure spirit and inner consciousness is the finding of pleasure in witnessing. The reality of it is the drinking of the wine of God, strained through the purity of loving-kindness from the sea of witnessing by the sacred spirits.

SS 530

'Drinking' is the receiving and embracing of the blessings of God as they arrive, and the benefiting from them by pure souls and inner beings of the mystics. It is said that this state is similar to the 'drinking' which arises from the wholesomeness and bounty of that which enters the heart through the lights of witnessing nearness to God.

Dho'n-Nun said, "The hearts of the loving ones will enter the sea of loving-kindness and there, with all the difficulties that they have, those hearts will drink a draught of wine, and all obstacles in the way of beholding the Beloved will be cleared away."

LT 372

Leave me alone! For my soul will not become sober
from drinking the nectar of purity.

Rumi

QUENCHING *(rayy)*

First 'tasting' *(dhauq)* obtains, then 'drinking', and finally 'quenching'. The wayfarers are led to the tasting of spiritual realities by the purity of their spiritual practice, and are led to drinking by the fidelity of their traversal of stations and are led to quenching by the duration of their moments in union. One with 'tasting' is in a state of semi-intoxication[1] *(tasâkor)*; one who 'drinks' is in a state of intoxication; and the one whose thirst is quenched is in a state of sobriety *(ṣaḥw)*.

Whosever's friendship is firm enjoys continuous drinking. When this state becomes permanent, his 'drinking' will not lead to intoxication. If one is sober in God, one loses one's enjoyment *(ḥaẓẓ)* and whatever happens to one will not affect or change one. Furthermore, whenever one's inner consciousness is purified, one's drinking will not be diminished; and one whose drinking has become his sustenance, becomes impatient and unable to survive without it.

> I drank love, cup after cup,
> And the wine never finished, nor was my thirst quenched.

They say that Yaḥya ebn Mo'âdh Râzi wrote to Bâyazid Basṭâmi, telling him of someone whose thirst would be quenched forever after drinking one pitcher of wine. Bâyazid wrote back, saying that this was a remarkably weak state, for he knew of one who could drink all the seas in the world and yet never have his fill, always craving more.

RQ 114

Ruzbehân conceives of 'quenching' as the fifth station of the lovers:

'Quenching' is experienced by those lovers who enjoy perpetual union continual drinking and eternal time *(yasarmado waqtahu)* in contemplation, whose mystical state and ectasy are so fervent as to be characterised by 'sobriety after intoxication' *(aṣ-ṣaḥw ba'da's-sokr)*. Here the lover, having found God after the realization of His attributes, subsists in Him through Him, unmoved by either intoxication or affliction. His thirst has been 'quenched' through annihilation in Eternity *(qedam)* and through effacement in pre-eternity *(azal)* through pre-eternity. Unable to find repose in God despite his thirst for Him, the lover's 'quenching' stems from neither an inhibited drinking-capacity, nor shortage of wine, nor diminished craving, but from the realisation of annihilation of self *(fanâ)* in subsistence in God *(baqâ')* and subsistence in God through annihilation of self. At this stage the garments of everlasting duration are instilled in pre-eternity and the garments of pre-eternity are

1. See the author's *Sufism: Fear and Hope....* p. 77.

curtailed in everlasting duration.

In this early stage the lover experiences 'quenching' through the taste of ecstasy *(dhauqo'l-wajd);* in its intermediate stage it is experienced as drinking in the pure presence of the moment *(shorbo ṣafâ'e'l-waqt),* and in the final stage it is realised as union with God within God through annihilation and subsistence.

A Sufi master stated that, "One who experiences drinking is in intoxication, and one who realises quenching is in sobriety."

The gnostic said, "When the wayfarer has become established in contemplation through annihilation therein, so that it permanently subsists within him, then his thirst is quenched and he possesses delight. However, once he has been annihilated by God in God so that no trace of his temporal nature taints his eternal being, his thirst then can never be quenched, for the oceans of pre-eternity are endless, and the drinking of those who are absorbed in divine union is everlasting!"

MA 118

Whenever the billowing of the waves of the attributes, rolling out of the seas of the Essence, causes a flood of theophanies of the divine names to flow into the rivers of the essences *(a'yân)* of created things and the waters of divine gnosis to surge into the streams of the sources of creation, the one receiving this grace becomes satisfied by drinking these waters, or at least, feels that his thirst is quenched.

> He cannot but say that his thirst is quenched.
> That which he sought, he has utterly become.

Those who enjoy friendship with God call this station 'thirst that is quenched', and the one at this station is called the 'quenched one'. This is the stage of the wayfarer who has the end of the Path in sight and for whom the limited life of the world is exposed, such that he has become an advocate of 'quenching' and cyclic recurrence. He believes in the cycle of days and months and contemplates the recurrence of theophanies. However, our friends on the path do not believe in cyclic recurrence. They regard each day and night as something new, saying that God manifests theophany in every individual and never repeats the theophany.

> The limits of our sea cannot be seen;
> Every moment it displays another wave.

'Tasting' is faith; 'drinking', knowledge, and 'quenching', spiritual state. 'Tasting' is particular to those who receive 'intuitive impulses' *(bawâdeh)*; 'drinking' is particular to those who experience 'auroral illumination' *(tawâle')*, 'flashes' *(lawâ'eḥ)*[1] and 'effulgence' *(lawâme')*; and 'quenching' is particular to those undergoing states. This view was based on the opinion that states are lasting and that which is not lasting is not a state, but rather 'effulgence' or 'auroral illumination'.

AM 528

'Tasting' is the initial experience of a theophany. Each theophany has an inital stage which is the 'tasting' of that theophany. Divine theophany confers 'tasting' either through forms or through spiritual realities *(ma'nâ)*. If 'tasting' is conferred through forms, it causes imaginary 'tasting', and if conferred through spiritual realities, that is, through the divine names, it causes 'tasting' on the part of the intellect. The 'tasting' on the part of the intellect affects the heart, while that of imagination affects the *nafs*. The former encourages austerities of the *nafs,* while the latter urges bodily effort. On the other hand, in the case of theophany of the Essence through the Essence in the Essence:

> The wave, stream, bubble and sea do not exist;
> Not only is there no tasting, but no one who may taste.

However, if one goes to take a second draught, it is called 'drinking'; and if one has a third, it is known as 'quenching'.

RSh III 262

'Tasting' signifies the wayfarer's initial experience of themanifestations of God's acts; 'drinking' is the experience of the effect of the intermediate stage of the manifestations of God's attributes; 'quenching' is the experience of the final state of the manifestation of God's acts by the intellect of the wayfarer and is the experience of the final stage of the manifestations of God's attributes by the hearts of gnostics.

MA 47

1. See the author's *Spiritual Poverty in Sufism*, p. 65-80.

'Yearning' is said to represent the heart's strong inclination *(mail)* and impatience to behold the Beloved.

> What is yearning? It is to come out of yourself;
> If you hope for the musk, first you must bleed.
>
> MN 42

> I'll send you epigrams and poems set to music,
> Till the minstrels inform you of my yearning for you.
>
> Ḥâfeẓ

> I wailed so much in yearning for her that I made
> my neighbour ill;
> Still the eye of my good fortune did not wake:
> What can I do?
>
> 'Erâqi

> Everyone abandons their hearts
> when seeking you through yearning;
> At dawn singing is heard from your roof.
>
> Sanâ'i

> The earth you tread is my sky, your poison my antidote;
> The yearning of my inner consciousness is the joy
> of my brooding heart.
>
> Rumi

'Yearning' is said to represent the distress experienced in seeking the Beloved when He has been lost. When He is found, the distress is relieved. Love, though, remains constant and rather then diminishing upon attaining the Beloved, increases.

EE 54

'Yearning' is said to symbolise the distress and movement of the heart toward the Beloved, the fervour of which abates once the

 Beloved is attained. In contrast love and pain increase with union. With every blandishment in the course of union, loving-kindness and love increase. 'Yearning' occurs during moments of estrangement, while love appeals for further presence at every breath due to the annihilation of the lover in the Beloved.

TT 211

From the point of view of the followers of the Path 'yearning' represents the heart's excitement *(hayajân)* while remembering the Beloved. Certain proponents of austerity maintain that 'yearning' in the heart of a lover is like the wick of a lamp and that love is the oil aflame.

One authority has held that 'yearning' is the substance of loving-kindness and that love is its embodiment. Furthermore, there is a saying that whoever "yearns for God grows intimate with Him; and whoever enjoys intimacy is in rapture; and whoever is in rapture attains union; and whoever is in union achieves conjunction *(etteṣâl)*; and whoever is in conjunction is fortunate, and to him a blessed return to God!"

When Abu 'Ali [Daqqâq] was asked about the difference between 'yearning' and 'longing' *(eshtiyâq)*, he replied, "Yearning is allayed with beholding [the Beloved], whereas 'longing' does not abate with beholding; it increases, in fact many times over."

In the book, *The Epitome of the Path (Majma' as-soluk)*, it says, "One of the states of loving kindness is 'yearning', which arises in the lover. The occurrence of yearning, following loving-kindness, is one of the divine bounties and cannot be acquired. Yearning which comes of loving-kindness is like asceticism which follows repentance. When repentance is established, asceticism appears, just as when loving-kindness is established, yearning appears."

Abu 'Othmân said, "Yearning is the fruit of loving-kindness; whoever loves God yearns to encounter Him."

KF 770

In the early stages, 'yearning' is the longing for paradise and for that which is divinely promised as heavenly reward. In the final stages, 'yearning' is longing for attainment of the vision of God in every theophany and throughout the universe.

RSh IV 179

'Yearning' refers to the attraction of the heart towards beholding the Beloved.

TJ 87

'Yearning' is the heart's infatuation *(hayamân)* in the moment of remembrance of the Beloved.

AF 53

LONGING *(eshtiyâq)*

Although the literal meaning of 'longing' is 'being desirous', in Sufi terminology the term signifies the profound 'feeling' *(tamâyol)* of the lover for the Beloved which does not change in union or separation.

When Ḥâfeẓ was writing this poem, full of distress,
The bird of his thoughts had fallen into the
    trap of longing.

Ḥâfeẓ

O soul, in longing for you,
    my heart came close to death;
Come, for I cannot go on
    bearing this sadness for you.

'Erâqi

Almighty god, do not burn me,
    for in longing for your door,
I have developed a great melancholy.

'Aṭṭâr

'Longing' signifies the inward attraction of the lover toward the Beloved while in the state of union, for the attainment of greater and lasting pleasure *(ledhdhat)*.

TJ 17

'Longing' is said to symbolise the height of unrest in the fullness of inclination, the totality of seeking, and continuous love, in such a way that attainment and non-attainment are the same. 'Longing' neither abates in attainment nor increases in non-attainment. On the contrary, it is a state which is eternal; it is the highest of the levels of loving-kindness, not subject to increase, decrease, or transformation, whether in the engagement of 'witnessing' or the disengagement of 'striving'.

EE 55

'Longing' is said to symbolise the height of the heart's unrest in its fundamental inclination towards the Prime Source. This longing has various levels. The beginning of 'longing' for the sincere ones occurs as the heart reaches the point where the seeker on the path becomes detached from everything, when his distress and irresolution are increasing, and when he is detached from the attainment of that which is desirable or the avoidance of that which is undesirable. This is the first stage of the love of the sincere.

They will welcome unbelief or faith,
So that the Beloved will open the door for them.
If you are truly a seeker, you must seek in this manner;
If you but claim to seek, you merely desire.

This 'longing' reaches a stage where consciousness of perfect desire and longing for the Beloved are experienced. This kind of 'longing' is manifested sometimes in the form of the lover and sometimes in that of the Beloved; it is experienced at the levels of the inner consciousness *(serr)* and the spirit *(ruḥ)* of the wayfarer.

You are all longing and desire;
    No, I am wrong,
Since in your subtlety both longing and desire
    are made restless and crazy by you.

When this 'longing' at its perfect level takes the form of love, to the extent that union and separation, faith and unbelief are the same to the lover, Majnun sees Laili[1] perpetually with him, as one absolutely integrated being, one spirit in two bodies, and he sees

1. The lover and the beloved from Neẓâmi's epic poem.

nothing in the whole of existence but the Beloved. This level occurs at the final point of the stage of the transconscious *(khafi)*.

TT 170

According to Ruzbehân, there are two types of 'longing', the first being the 'longing' of the 'longing one' *(moshtâq)* of which he writes:

The primary stage of 'yearning' is 'loving-kindness'; its intermediate stage, affectionate love *(ṣabâbat)*, and the final stage, 'longing', which represents the ultimate limit of perfection. When the 'yearning one' *(shâ'eq)* attains the station of 'longing', God longs for him. At this point he attains pre-eternal 'longing' which does not abate, for it is inconsolable, even if the one affected by it attains the station of 'beholding' *(didâr)*.

Nasrâbâdi said, "Everyone experiences the station of yearning for God, but not that of 'longing', for one who becomes established in the sites of longing, first becomes distracted therein, and finally no trace of existence may be seen in him. This state causes the realisation that yearning is constant during the vision of nearness [to God] after the attainment of union.

The gnostic said, "Longing means the flaring up of the fire of yearning through the light of sincerity."

MA 115

The second type of 'longing' to which Ruzbehân addresses himself is the 'longing' of the wayfarer:

'Longing' is an attribute of the spirit that wanders through the pavilions of detachment from the world. This occurs after the spirit has perceived the light of pure power which appears in the environs of the sacred precincts of the invisible cosmos and has become acquainted with the holy bolts of lightning and the aroma of the flower of intimacy and has taken flight on its own from the source of phenomenal nature *(feṭrat)* towards he realm of unity. The Prophet alluded to this mystery when he said, "Indeed I feel the breath of the Merciful from the direction of Yemen."[1]

MA 30

1. Foruzânfar, No. 195.

Zephyr, if you have a remedy, now is the moment,
For my longing pain has design, upon my soul.

Ḥâfeẓ

CRAVING *(wala')*

'Craving', in Sufi terminology, signifies intense and lasting inclination. When the attraction of the heart toward the Sought One grows strong and becomes lasting it is called 'craving'. This is one of the first levels of devotion.

INFATUATION *(hayamân)*

'Infatuation' represents the bewilderment of the spirit during the realisation of unity.

SS 633

'Infatuation' refers to the bewilderment which the theophanies of Absolute Majesty and Beauty cause in infatuated angels *(malâ'ek-e mohayyama)* and those human beings who are attracted to God; and all those who are attracted to God benefit in different degrees.

RSh 292

'Infatuation' arises from an excess of 'love', while 'love' is an excess of 'loving-kindness', and 'loving-kindness' is the basis of the creation of the world. 'Loving-kindness' in turn arises from theophanies which are infusions from the Absolute Beauty.

RSh IV 399

'Infatuation' is one of the stations of the lovers. When the thirst of yearning overcomes the lover and he experiences a little of the beauty of union, he attains 'infatuation' by drinking from the chalice of loving-kindness and by the increase of nearness in nearness [to God]. When his spiritual moment becomes purified in loving-kindness, some of the lights of uniqueness become revealed to him, and he settles in the valleys of knowing the Eternal, until the flooding waters of the rivers of the attributes sweep him away, so that he vanishes from view.

The gnostic said, "Infatuation symbolises the experience of Enravishment *(walah)* in the heart of the lover, characterised by distraction in the station of annihilation in the Beloved."

MA 88

Anṣâri begins his description of 'infatuation' by quoting the Koran: "And Moses fell swooning" (VII: 143), and continues as follows: 'Infatuation' signifies loss of restraint due to amazement and bewilderment. Its duration is more firmly grounded and appears in more forms than that of 'bedazzlement' *(dahshat)*; it has three degrees.

The first degree occurs when the first flashes of grace *(loṭf)* are experienced by the devotee at the beginning of the path. As a result of this the devotee understands the baseness of his station and his fundamental worthlessness.

The second degree occurs when the billowing waves of 'realisation' are experienced. It is then that the first evidences thereof apear, its wonders follow, and its lights shine forth.

The third degree occurs when one has become realised in the essence of the Eternal, enjoying the direct observation of the Monarch of pre-eternity and drowing in the sea of visionary revelation.

MS 163

GRACE *(loṭf)*

'Grace' is said to represent the nurturing of the gnostic through supportiveness and companionship.

EE 55

'Grace' symbolises the Beloved's nurturing of the lover through sympathy and kindness, sincerity and supportiveness.

Ḥâfeẓ writes:

Who am I, that I should be
    the object of your fragrant attention?
You bestow graces; the dust of your doorway
    is the crown upon my head!

TT 226

In Sufi terminology, 'grace' signifies the Beloved's nurturing of the lover by His sympathy and supportiveness, so that the lover may attain full strength and vigour in order to behold His beauty.

KF 1299

Love flirted in such a way
that it diverted the cleric from his path;
And the friend bestowed such grace
that the foe took flight.

Ḥâfeẓ

Where is all the grace
I saw upon your face each night?
And where are those sweet stories
that I heard you tell each night?

Rumi

We have fallen upon the threshold of your grace;
We have placed our hopes in your mercy.

'Erâqi

Abo'l-Ḥasan Kharaqâni said, "Almighty God bestowed grace on His friends, and God's grace is like His deception *(makr)*.

TA 691

WRATH *(qahr)*

The Prophetic Tradition, "He [God] steps upon hell..."[1] refers to the luminous unveiling of Eternity's proximity to the transient actions of created beings. The action *(fe'l)* of God, is God's very character *(na'ṭ)*: His character is His descriptive quality *(ṣefat)*, and His descriptive quality is His essence *(dhât)*; although related, each of these is unique in every respect. God displays himself from wrath unto wrath; the wrath of eternity, which is His innermost recess, prevails over the wrath of His action, until the wrath of His action is surfeited with the wrath of eternity. Hell is an action of God, but such action is not left of its own activity; rather, the Eternal Being prevails until all activity but that of eternity is obliterated. God is the essence of every atom, but appears to the spirit's infirm perception as

1. Cited by Ruzbehân, SS 62.

'eternity'. God sheds his grace upon each atom, according to its particular nature, so that he may bear the atom away from itself through His love. Then, when the atom no longer exists, it is said to be obliterated. All of these things bear only the colour of the divine actions. God himself transcends the approach of created beings. In the wrath of eternity, the self-conscious intellect becomes charmed and tantalised, for God appears to the lovers in the beauteous splendour of every atom.

SS 65

If he speaks with wrath on the Day of Judgement,
Even prophets may not be pardoned;
Ask him, therefore, to unveil his grace,
So that even the oppressors may hope for forgiveness.

Sa'di

'Wrath' and 'grace' are employed by the Sufis to describe their own states. By 'wrath' they mean the reinforcement given to them by God in annihilating their desires and in restraining the *nafs* from its concupiscence, without any will on their part. By 'grace' they mean God's help given to their inner consciousness, their continuace of contemplation and to the degree of steadfastness in the permanence of their mystical states. The adherents of grace have maintained that divine favour is the attainment of one's desires while others maintain that God's favour is this: that God, through His will, should restrain a man from his own will and should overpower him with will-lessness, so that if he were to be thirsty and plunge into a river, the river would become dry.

It is related that in Baghdad there were two eminent darvishes, one a proponent of wrath and the other a proponent of grace. They were constantly in dispute with one another, each preferring his own state to that of the other. One asserted that grace from God towards the devotee is the noblest of all things, citing the Koranic verse, "God is gracious to His servants" (XLII: 19), while the other maintained that wrath from God towards the devotee is better, quoting the verse, "He is omnipotent over His servants" (VI: 18, 61). This discussion went on and on between them, until the proponent of grace decided to go to Mecca. He set out through the desert, yet never reached his destination. For many years there was no news of him until at last he was seen by a traveller on the road between Mecca and Baghdad. He said to the traveller, "O my brother, when you return to Iraq, tell that friend of mine at Karkh[1] that if he wishes to see a desert with all its hardships like Karkh of Baghdad with all its marvels, let him come here, for the desert is Karkh to me."

When the traveller arrived at Karkh, he delivered this message to the other darvish, who said, "When you go back, say that there is nothing superior in the fact that the desert has been made like Karkh to him, in order that he may not flee the court of God. The superiority lies in the fact that Karkh, with all its wondrous opulence, has been made a painful desert for me, so that I might be happy therein."

It is related that Shebli, in his secret converse with God, used to say, "O Lord, even if You should make the sky a collar round my neck, the earth chained to my foot, and the whole universe athirst for my blood, I shall not turn away from you!"

My master also related the following story: "One year a meeting of the saints of God took place in the middle of the desert, and I accompanied my master, Ḥosri, to that place. I saw some arriving on thoroughbred camels, some borne on thrones and some come flying, but Ḥosri took no notice of the likes of these. Then, a youth approached wearing tattered sandals and carrying a broken staff, his legs hardly able to support him, his head bare, and his body emaciated. As soon as he appeared Ḥosri ran to him and escorted him to a lofty seat. I was amazed and afterwards, when I questioned my master about the youth, he said, 'He is a friend of God who does not adhere to God's friendship; rather, God's friendship adheres to him. He is not concerned with miracles'."

In short, that which we choose for ourselves is noxious to us; I desire that God should desire for me, and therein to preserve me from the evil thereof and save me from the wickedness of my soul. If He subjects me to wrath, I do not desire grace; and if he showers grace upon me, I do not wish for wrath; I have no choice over what He chooses.[2]

KM 492-494

DELICATENESS (*ẓarâfat*)

'Delicateness' signifies the appearance of lights devoid of all material form during contemplation.

EE 55

1. A section of Baghdad.
2. Nicholson's translation with minor changes, *op. cit.* p. 377-79.

'Sauciness' represents the emanation of auroral illumination *(tawâle')* and effulgence *(lawâme')* of the lights from God through matter.

EE 55

This charm and sauciness is not without reason;
This rebellion and prankishness, from where has
it come?

Fakhr Banâketi

IMPUDENCE *(shukhi)*

'Impudence' is said to represent the abundance of [divine] favour.

EE 55

'Impudence' is said to symbolise existential manifestations through matter.

Impudently, he gives life to water and earth;
With his breath he sets the heavens on fire.

TT 211

'Impudence' is said to signify abundance of favour through the manifestation of different forms of God's action.

KF 1559

'Impudence' signifies divine attraction.

SGR 581

I'm content with that winsome amorous gesture
which she,
Through impudence, has transformed each promise
of torment to fidelity.

Kamâl Khojandi

That which they say is beautiful in your face, is so,
And that which is impudent and graceful in your eyes,
is so too.

Sa'di

AMOROUS GLANCE *(kereshmeh)*

'Amorous glance' is said to represent [divine] favour.

EE 55

'Amorous glance' refers to the grace of the Beloved which may be conveyed by a glance of the eye.

LG II 4

'Amorous glance' is said to symbolise God's favour conferred upon the wayfarer in such a way as to cause his heart to be totally attracted to God.

With one amorous glance
you can set our work aright;
Why do you not provide
help for the helpless ones?

TT 224

'Amorous glance' is said to signify the theophany of Majesty *(jalâl)*.

KF 1561

Lovingly bear reproach from the beautiful friend,
Who, with one amorous glance, makes up for a
hundred torments.

Ḥâfeẓ

COQUETRY *(dalâl)*

In the terminology of the wayfarers of the path, 'coquetry' is said to represent the agitation which is aroused in the wayfarer in the course of the unveiling of the Beloved due to the extreme love and mystical savour in his inner being. Although the wayfarer in this state is not as free of self as one who is intoxicated, he has no will of his own and in this state he expresses all that appears in his heart because of excessive agitation.

SGR 561

MANNER *(shiweh)*

'Manner' is said to represent the minimum of divine attraction which may obtain in every state of the wayfarer. However, in order that the wayfarer may not become proud because of its continuity, or broken because of its absence, it is sometimes present and sometimes not.[1]

EE 55

The manner of lover-slaying and exciting discord
Is the robe that is taylored to fit her figure.

Ḥâfeẓ

I am rapture; rapture is me; Venus plays my tune;
Let the love amongst the lovers display its manner
for me!

Rumi

FEIGNED DISDAIN *(nâz)*

'Feigned disdain' represents the Beloved's strengthening of the lover.

EE 56

'Feigned disdain' is said to symbolise self-esteem and veiling on the part of the Beloved for the purpose of arousing the fullest desire and the continuance of loving-kindness in the development of the lover, so that his seeking may undergo steady increase and he may all the sooner pass through the degrees of advancement and ascent to reach the fundamental goal.

TT 231

1. Cf. KF 1559.

'Feigned disdain' signifies the Beloved's strengthening of the lover who is full of sadness and sorrow.

KF 1563

They never match, our need and the feigned disdain
of the beauty of the friend;
Happy is the one who has the fortune
to know truly the disdainful friends.

Ḥâfeẓ

If you would reduce the cruelty of your feigned disdain,
I am sure that your beauty would not lessen.

'Erâqi

Everyone seeks your feigned disdain,
but no one needs it like me;
Everyone wants your insults,
but no one prays for them like me.

Kamâl Khojandi

SPIRITUAL NEED *(niyâz)*[1]

'Spiritual need' is the lover's expression of abjectness and impoverishment when he is confronted with the self-sufficiency of the Beloved; it demonstrates the profundity and stability of his loving-kindness. It also represents his outward appeal for an increase in grace and hidden favour from the Beloved. As Ḥâfeẓ writes:

The difference between lover
and Beloved is considerable;
When the latter is disdainful,
then you must be spiritually needy.

TT 234

1. In some cases *niyâz* may be rendered as 'supplication'.

Abo'l-Ḥasan Kharaqâni said, "God called to my heart, saying, 'Wherever there is supplication, I am the Object; wherever there are pretensions, the world is the object.'"

NO 19

Abu Sa'id Abe'l-Khair said, "One must have 'spiritual need' for there is no shorter way to God for the devotee; if it passes through solid rock, water springs forth. 'Spiritual need' is fundamental for Sufis; it is the bestowal of God's mercy upon them.

AT 264

A Sufi asked Abu Sa'id Abe'l-Khair, "O master, what kind of burning is this in our hearts?" He replied, "This is called the fire of spiritual need; God has created two types of fire: a living fire and a dead fire. The living fire is the fire of spiritual need which He has placed in the hearts of devotees so as to burn their *nafs*; it is an illuminating fire. When the *nafs* is consumed, this fire will turn into the fire of yearning which never dies."

AT 308

You"ll be freed from the trap of your being,
when, through spiritual need,
You're trodden underfoot, like a mat,
in the mosque and the winehouse.

Sanâ'i

The ascetic with his vanity and prayer,
and I with my drundenness and spiritual need;
You must choose to whom you bestow your favour.

Ḥâfeẓ

Do not kill me,
for my spiritual need is of use to you!
If I cease to exist,
with whom will your beauty be disdainful?

'Erâqi

'Apology' is one of the stations of the sincere ones.

The transgressions of the gnostics are a cause for their closeness [to God]. This is so in the following manner. Whenever they find themselves in the seas of trial, they glorify God's name in bewildernment. Once they have understood the nature of their transgressions, they appeal to God through God for help, whereupon He releases them from their transgressions by His benevolent hand. Once they have been delivered from the predicament of those trangressions, they find themselves before the door of God's grandeur. There, having gained awareness of their transgressions and become humbled in shame, they offer 'apology' to God through God for these transgressions, whereupon they are annihilated by the fury of Divine Majesty.

God opens the doors of His munificence and scatters the jewels of the seas of Eternity upon their inner consciousness, causing them to utter 'apologies' and motivating their impoverished inner consciousness towards Himself, so that they cry, "Our Lord, we have wronged ourselves!" (VII: 23); and he replies, "I love you and accept your apologies" as in the verse, "Indeed, God loves those that turn to Him" (II: 222), and "He had access to our presence and a happy journey's end" (XXXVIII: 25).

It is clear that from God's point of view the transgressions of a sincere human being engender closeness and intensify nearness [to God]. For this reason God said, "O devotees of Mine, you are forgiven and are not misled. My will has preceded your transgressions. How could you avert such a decree? Thus, in the disclosing of My munificent face, I Myself offer 'apology' to you and your friends for having set your sinning in motion." Thereupon, they shall be "Firmly established in the favour of a Mighty King" (LVI: 55) in the circle of the angels, who enter to attend them from every door, saying, "Peace be upon you for having preserved. And passing sweet will be the sequel of the heavenly home" (XIII: 24).

The explanation of this matter of God's 'apology', and the fact that the devotee's volition is derived from God's own pre-existing will, appears in the passage, "Now, you do not will unless God wills" (LXXXVI: 30).

As the Prophet said, "Whenever God loves a devotee, He does not allow his sinning to harm him."

The gnostic said, "The gnostic's realisation of his own ignorance is his 'apology'. The expression of the solitary God is His participation in the will of created beings, and herein lies His 'apology' to the gnostic."

MA 74

I prostrate to her and apologise for her step
which cruly trod upon me,
As if I were dust on the path.

Ḥâfeẓ

WANTS *(ḥâjat)*

In the *Majma' as-soluk (Epitome of the Path),* it states that the 'basic necessities' *(ḍharurât)* represent that without which a person cannot subsist and that to which the *nafs* is entitled. The 'minimal wants', on the other hand, are said to represent those things without which a person may subsist, though they are needed, such as outer garments covering one's underclothing and footware. Finally, 'excess' *(foḍhul)* is said to represent that which goes beyond these two, and that is limitless. Accordingly, the novice disciple must renounce both 'minimal wants' and 'excess' and make do with 'necessities'.

KF 285

If you seek beholding, you must find it in the heart;
You cannot supplicate for wants, like Moses on
Mount Sinai.

Maghrebi

AMOROUS GLANCE *(ghamza)*

The 'amorous glance' is said to stand for the emanation of grace and inner attraction which are experienced by the wayfarer.

KF 1560

The 'amorous glance' is said to symbolise the theophany through forms which causes the wayfarer to become annihilated. It may also be applied to the theophany through forms in itself, without the involvement of annihilation, as well as to the attraction which is experienced in the early stages of the Path.

The Saqi's amorous glance brandished a sword [1]
to plunder wisdom;
The tresses of the soul of souls laid a trap
to catch the heart.

TT 219

The 'amorous glance' is the Beloved's fluttering of the eyes in the course of captivation and flirtation. The closing of the eyes alludes to the absence of favour and the opening of them indicates consideration and graciousness. These two qualities serve to evoke fear and hope in the lover:

Each amorous glance of hers became trap and bait,
And through her, every corner became a winehouse.

The 'amorous glance' may also indicate self-sufficiency and the absence of favour [on the part of the Beloved]:

With her amorous glance she plunders our being;
With her kisses she restores it again.

SGR 570

The heart is enmeshed in the trap of our tresses;
slay it through your amorous glance,
For this is what it deserves!

Ḥâfeẓ

There are ambushes everywhere due to
your blood-thirsty amorous glance
Not a night goes by without this occuring
in a hundred places.

'Erâqi

1. The 'eyebrow'; see under *Sufi Symbolism*, Vol. I, p. 3-6.

An amorous glance, while beholding your face,
    is better than a skirtful of gold;
If one were to behold you, who'd care about gold?

Rumi

Her conjuring amorous glance
    comes from the eyes of the angel-faced
And steals people's hearts with a hundred spells.

Maghrebi

AMOROUS GESTURE (*'eshwa)*

In the terminology of the lover, the 'amorous gesture' is said to signify theophany of the Beauty.

KF 1075

The 'amorous gesture' is said to symbolise the theophanies of Beauty which appear in divine manifestations.

With an amorous glance her eyes steal the heart;
With amorous gestures her ruby lips quicken souls.

TT 216

What a shame that all your life
    has been devoted to amorous gestures!
Who today is so alluring
    and who responds the way you do?

'Aṭṭâr

Who is not drunk in you?
    Who does not worship your amorous gestures?
Who is not a pawn in your hand?
    Scatter, then, munificence with that hand!

Rumi

The palate of my soul is bitter
    from waiting so long for the friend;
Show me the amorous gestures
    from your sweet and sugary lips!

Ḥâfeẓ

LOVE-CRAZED *(shaidâ)*

The term 'love-crazed' is said to describe those who are attracted and who experience yearning.

KF 1559

I see no one among the elect or the masses,
Privy to the secret of my love-crazed heart.

Ḥâfeẓ

I became love-crazed when my beautiful mistress
    like the new moon,
Revealed an eyebrow, displayed herself
    then closed the door.

Ḥâfeẓ

The entire world is enraptured
    and love-crazed for you;
But no one is enraptured
    and love-crazed like me!

'Erâqi

FIDELITY *(wafâ')*

'Fidelity' signifies the maintenance of friendship and one's pledge [to God].

'Fidelity' is said to represent pre-eternal favour and is not dependent on the performance of good works or the avoidance of transgressions.

EE 56

'Fidelity' is said to symbolise observance of the pre-eternal pledges that the permanent archetypes *(a'yân-e thâbeta)* and spirits made with God, as in the Koranic verse, "Fulfill your part of the covenant and I shall fulfill my part of the covenant" (II: 40). This is illustrated by Rumi thus:[1]

Heed the call to be "faithful to the pledge with me,"
So that the companion will honour his with you.
You are blind to God's fidelity; you have not heard,
"Remember Me; I shall remember you."[2]

TT 235

'Aṭṭâr's wounded heart
Could not receive a better cure from you
than your fidelity.

'Aṭṭâr

In the *Laṭâ'ef al-loghât (The Subtleties of Words)*, it states, "In Sufi terminology, 'fidelity' signifies [for the ordinary person] the fulfillment of the promise made on the Day of the Covenant (Koran, VII: 172) for the one who has honoured his pledge in maintaining faith and observing devotional practices in desiring heaven and fearing hell; while for the elect, it represents a servanthood which understands the divine command as a command and not in terms of desiring heaven and fearing hell. For the elect of the elect, it is unqualified servanthood."

KF 1562

'Fidelity' signifies perseverence in maintaining the way of fellowship and in honouring commitments to one's associates.

TJ 171

'Fidelity' is ultimate harmony and compliance with one's promise. It is the only capital of the 'longing ones' and the foundation for lovers. It is the substance of sincerity and the ornament of the elect, the concealing of one's secrets and the non-revealing of the

1. MM V: 1182-1183.
2. Koran II: 152.

secrets of the Friend. The 'fidelity of the ordinary' is outward and that of the Friend, inward. The 'fidelity of the ordinary' requires the presence of the Friend, while that of the elect subsists in remembrance of the Friend. While the former prevents the impairment of friendship the latter permits no replacement of friendship. While the former does not flee from torment, the latter does not rely on gifts. The former is the work of men, while the latter is the work of the unwise. The former is a pledge made through God's favour, with Adam as proxy, that there is no alternative to boundsmanship, while the latter is a pledge of divine friendship, which is beyond words.

RJ 126

Lovers have no expectation from their Beloved
in return for their fidelity;
And they never run away
from his cruelty.

'Erâqi

No one matches our companion
in good nature and fidelity;
This statement of ours
cannot be rebutted.

Ḥâfeẓ

If you are sympathetic, it is favour;
if you are oppressive, it is munificence.
O my Beloved, everything from you is fine,
be it cruelty or fidelity.

Hâtef Eṣfahâni

Ma'ruf Karkhi said, "The true nature of fidelity is the awakening of the inner consciousness from the sleep of neglect, and the liberation from harmful thoughts."[1]

TA 327

1. Cf. TS(S) 77.

Abo'l-Ḥasan Kharaqâni said, "When you see yourself with God, that is fidelity; and when you see God with yourself, that is annihilation."

TA 705

When Abo'l-Ḥasan Armawi was asked what 'fidelity' was, he replied, "It is not to return to something you have renounced." Again they asked, "This is the fidelity of the ordinary; what is that of the elect?" He answered, "To know why you have renounced it."

TS(A) 532

When Shebli was asked about fidelity, he said, "Fidelity is frankness of speech and the steeping of one's inner being in sincerity."

TS(S) 345

PURITY *(ṣafâ')*

In Sufi terminology, 'purity' is said to characterise a wayfarer who is free of falseness and the turbidity of ego-consciousness, such that there is no difference between his inward and outward being.

The true meaning of 'purity' is to be separate from creation and to be characterised by the attributes of Reality.

SS 561

In the early stages, 'purity' is that of knowledge, specifically with respect to actions and the preparation of the *nafs* for the traversal of the path; in the final stages, it is that of concentration *(jam')* through the vision of God without the creation.

RSh IV 180

'Purity' is said to represent the heart's becoming cleansed through asceticism.

> Do not turn from the door of the pure ones, O heart!
> Whoever is distant is close to God by way of this door.

TT 212

We are Sufis of the dais of purity;
Without sense of self, we are with God.

'Aṭṭâr

The lovers opened the door
of the realm of purity
Into the chamber of existence.

'Erâqi

Seek purity of heart to see the face,
for no one looks upon the face
Until he has first experienced
the water of purity.

'Aṭṭâr

O Beloved, release your wine
and grant a little to us!
Give to our compounded sadness,
purity through a sip.

Rumi

Through the purity of her countenance
the soul's retreat is pure,
And the radiant light of her face
illumines the house of her heart.

Maghrebi

Purity has a principle and a corollary; its principle is the severence of the heart from that which is other than God and its corollary is detachment from the deceiving world.

KM 35

The sixty-second field is that of purity, which arises from the field of sincerity. As it says in the Koran "They quailed not, for whatever befell them in God's Way" (III: 146).

The 'pure ones' are of three categories. The first consists of the angels who are free of lust, void of ill-thinking, and immune from forgetfulness. The second consists of the prophets, who are free from retrogression, void of embellishment and immune from sinning. The third consists of the 'pure believers', who, though lower than the prophets, are liberated from domination by the *nafs*, linked to God in their hearts, and adorned by gnosis of Him in their inner consciousness.

SM 337

'Purity' signifies the truths of the present moment in which one becomes unadulterated by human nature and free from consciousness of one's actions.

Jorairi said, "Contemplation of one's own purity is infidelity, because it is mixed with human nature and consciousness of one's own acts."

Ebn 'Aṭâ' said, "Do not be beguiled by the purity of servanthood, for therein lies the neglect of Lordship; the purity of servanthood is mixed with human nature and consciousness of one's own acts.

When Kattâni was asked about 'purity', he said, "It is the shedding of undesirable qualities."

LT 338

The Koran says, "In our eyes they are verily of the elect, the excellent" (XXXVIII: 47).

Generally, 'purity' represents liberation from impurity. In the folllowing passage though, it represents the elimination of fluctuation, and has three degrees. The first is 'purity of knowledge' *(ṣafâ-ye 'elm)*, which refines the approach to the path, gives hope for ultimate effort and corrects the aspiration of one who has set his sights. The second is 'purity of state' *(ṣafâ-ye ḥâl)* through which the manifestations of God's beauty become actualised through witnessing, the sweetness of spiritual comunion is tasted, and the existence of the world is forgotten. The last is the 'purity of union' *(ṣafâ-ye etteṣâl)*, which is to lose one's pleasure in service while consigning oneself to the deity, to lose interest in what is heard of the final stages of the path at the point when one begins to experience visual perception, and to comprehend the worthlessness of spiritual duties before the almightiness of pre-eternity.

MS 173

'Purity' is one of the stations of the sincere *(ṣeddiq)*.

The *nafs* has a 'purity' which is 'purity of nature'; the heart has a 'purity' which is 'purity of disposition'; the spirit has a 'purity' which is particular to itself; the intellect has a 'purity' which is 'purity of aptitude', and the outward form has a 'purity' which is 'purity of disposition'. When the *nafs* is at peace *(tama'nina)*, it becomes cleansed by the 'purity' of fear of God, which is the foundation of serenity as described in the verse, "O thou soul at peace,..." (LXXXIX: 27).

When the heart becomes purified through the purity of remembrance, it becomes cleansed through the serenity of remembrance, as is described in the verse, "Truly, in remembrance of God do hearts find rest" (XIII: 28).

When the spirit becomes purified by the lights of God, it becomes cleansed by the light of the unseen, spoken of in the Koran as "light upon light" (XXIV: 35).

When the intellect becomes purified by the light of God's signs, it becomes cleansed through the unveiling of divine acts, as described in the verse, "Lo! Herein truly are portents for men of thought" (XX: 54).

Finally, when the outward form becomes purified through the 'purity of devout actions', it bears the mark of angels and spiritual beings, as is said in the Koran, "You know them by their mark" (II: 273), and "Their mark is on their faces from the traces of prostration" (XLVIII: 29). When these attributes are perfected, the lamp of the heart becomes pure, and the 'purity of gnosis' gained from witnessing God descends upon it. The 'purity of gnosis' is the principle of all the attributes as indicated in the verse, "God guides to His light whom He wills" (XXIV: 35), and "We have made it a light whereby We guide whom We will" (XLII: 52).

The gnostic said, "Purity' signifies the purity of the intellect within the creation, the purity of devotional practice within the canon law, the purity of an attribute within Divine Reality, the purity of the angelic realm within the intellect, and the purity of witnessing within spirits, while the reality of 'purity' is the light of the unseen, which is manifested from God as a result of conviction and resolution."

MA 53

PURITY OF PURITY *(ṣafâ-ye ṣafâ')*

The 'purity of purity' signifies the revealing of the secrets of transitory things through the witnessing of God in a state of union, its reality being the shedding the conventions of worshipping the Lordship through the attainment of truths.

SS 562

Whenever the gnostic is cleansed by the lights of remembrance from everything other than the Remembered One, he will be in the station of 'purity'. However, this state will not be perfected, unless he is cleansed from the remembrance itself through the vision of the Remembered One.

The gnostic said, "The 'purity of purity' represents the purity of gnosis, which is higher than the purity of devotional practice."

MA 277

When Kattâni was asked about the 'purity of purity', he said, "It is the losing of states and stations in order to enter the final stages [of the path]. It is also the disclosure of the secrets of transitory things through the vision of God by God, continuously and without cause."

LT 338

TURBIDITY *(kodurat)*

'Turbidity' is one of the stations of the visionaries.

'Turbidity' is the intermingling of anguish and regret which belong to the realm of ignorance in the form of jealousy *(ghairat)*, which veils the sight of the visionary in such a way that he finds himself in a state of listlessness, which frightens him. This causes his inner consciousness and the inner consciousness of his inner consciousness to contract, and anxieties build up in his heart. He searches for his Beloved in the dust of this 'turbidity', but being unable to find Him, he helplessly seeks refuge in his Lord. Following this, the suns of the Essence and the moons of the attributes rise for him, re-opening the way of gnosis through the sweetness of loving-kindness. As the Koran says, "He draws them out of darkness into light"(II: 257).

Wâseṭi said, "I sought God in purity and found Him in turbidity."

The gnostic said, "Turbidity is the mist of ignorance, beyond which lie the lights of gnosis."

MA 173

Association with the Friend has cleared
turbidity from Ḥâfeẓ's heart;
Observe the purity of aspiration of the
immaculate ones and those pure in religion.

Ḥâfeẓ

CRUELTY *(jafâ')*

'Cruelty' is said to represent the shrouding of the heart of the wayfarer from perception and witnessing.

EE 56

'Cruelty' is said to symbolise the shrouding of the wayfarer's heart from the witnessing of the nuances of beauty, in order to try him.

Suppose that you subject
wretched me to your cruelty.
To whom can I appeal?
It is you who are the sovereign!

TT 187

What kind of an idol is she,
the monkish heart's cunning idol?
She wounds only the hearts
of lovers with the sword of cruelty

Sanâ'i

If you put me out of your regard,
that itself is a form of regard;
Whatever cruelty comes from you
is just another form of fidelity!

Kamâl Khojandi

A foe's approach is to be cruel;
O Lord, you are friend and beloved,
so do not be cruel!

Sa'di

God forbid that I should complain
of your cruelty and oppression!
Injustice from the subtle ones
is all grace and graciousness!

Ḥâfeẓ

How long must wretched 'Erâqi
put up with your cruelty?
Don't worry—your cruelty
will also pass.

'Erâqi

For God's sake, for how many days
and nights am I to scream,
Weep blood, and sigh and wail
because of your cruelty?

Hâtef Eṣfahâni

What offence have I committed
that you should throw me out again
And visit your cruelty
upon this innocent separated one?

Rumi

SINCERITY *(ṣedq)*

In the terminology of the wayfarers, 'sincerity' means to show yourself as you are and to be truthful with God and the creation, both outwardly and inwardly.

Though I exist in time, my sincere soul
Is praying constantly before your eyebrows.

Rumi

With sincerity I have aimed a thousand darts of prayer,
But till now I have not enjoyed a single hit.

Ḥâfeẓ

As the dawn gives up its life to the sun,
so in the path of your love, do the ones
Who, with sincerity and purity,
give up their souls to the sun of your visage.

'Aṭṭâr

In the early stages, 'sincerity' is expressed in words and deeds, while in the final ones, it is expressed in the obliteration of every trace of 'being' in the Essence of God.

RSh IV 175

'Sincerity' means to speak the truth even under threat of destruction.

TJ 89

'Sincerity' is the foundation for actions, being of the next rank below prophecy. Furthermore, the slightest 'sincerity' leads to the conformity of the inner consciousness and outward behaviour, that is to say, the integrity of the inward and outward 'being' of the wayfarer.

RQ 97

Jonaid said, "The true nature of 'sincerity' is in telling the truth in situations from which one can be saved only by lying."

RQ 330

'Sincerity' is truthfulness between the inward and outward being.

AF 52

When Bâyazid was asked how he had arrived at his station, he said, "I gathered up the things of this world and tied them up with the chain of satisfaction; I then placed them in the catapult of sincerity and hurled them into the sea of despair."

TA 199

'Sincerity' may refer to that of intention, speech or action.

'Sincerity in intention' is the constancy of purpose with attention to God in whatever enterprise is undertaken. 'Sincerity in speech' is an utterance which is consistent with the truth, even though it may lead to injury to property or to self. 'Sincerity in action' is to seek God's contentment in whatever is done, not in the pleasing of people.

For the wayfarers of the path, 'sincerity' is the conformity of inner consciousness and outward behaviour, involving both inward and outward constancy with God. Such constancy arises when nothing but God comes to the wayfarer's mind. One who is characterised by this quality, namely, being truthful inwardly and outwardly and abandoning consciousness of the creation in the continuity of witnessing God, is called 'sincere'.

Qoshairi said, "Sincerity means absence of disturbance in one's state's, absence of doubt in one's beliefs, and absence of defect in one's actions."

KF 847

A master, asked about 'sincerity', said "It is to do what you say you will do, to be what you show yourself to be, and to be what you claim to be."

KAM VIII 424

CANDOUR *(ṣedâqat)*

For the adherents of the path, 'candour' represents the equanimity of the heart, whether exposed to fidelity *(wafâ')* or cruelty *(jafâ')*, withholding or bestowal; it is one of the levels of 'loving-kindness'.

'Candour' has five degrees: The first is 'purity' *(ṣafâ')*, and is indicated by emnity with the *nafs* and passions, opposition to personal desires, renunciation of lust with a view to perfect contentment, and total detachment from the world.

The second degree involves 'jealousy' *(ghairat)*. Here the chivalrous lover *(javânmard)* becomes jealous, and is displeased if anyone else mentions the name of his Beloved, or if anyone else finds, or looks at his Beloved. In the final stage of this station, he becomes jealous of himself with respect to his Beloved. Shebli cried, "O Lord! Strike me blind, for You are greater and grander than anything my eyes deserve to see!"

The third degree is 'longing' *(eshtiyâq)*, in which station the fire of yearning and desire flares up and begins to blaze.

The fourth is 'remembrance' *(dhekr)* of the Beloved, as in "Whoever loves something, remembers it more."[1] The fifth is 'bewilderment' *(taḥayyor)* concerning which the Prophet invoked God thus: "O Guide of the bewildered!" referring to 'bewilderment' in the first stages, and prayed, "Lord, increase my bewilderment!"[2] referring to that of the final stages. Do you know how this station differs from the first? This station is so high that it is impossible to convey what it is like. The Beloved is Himself so sublime that attainment of Him can only take place through bewilderment and amazement.

KF 850

DIVINE SINCERITY *(ṣadiqiyat)*

'Divine sincerity' is the highest degree of 'divine friendship' *(welâyat)* and the next below 'prophecy' *(nabowwat)*. Whoever ascends from this station proceeds directly to 'prophecy'.

KF 847

PATIENCE *(ṣabr)*

In Sufi terminology, 'patience' signifies the tolerance of afflictions and trials and the abandonment of complaint regarding these things.

If your patience is like that of Noah
in the sadness of the storm,
Affliction will leave you and the hopes
of a thousand years will be fulfilled.

Ḥâfeẓ

When we saw you, like a flower in the hands of others,
We tore the cloak of patience into shreds.

Kamâl Khojandi

1. Cited in the author's *Traditions of the Prophet*, Vol. II, p. 25.
2. These statements are not listed as *ahâdith* in Wensinck's *Concordance of Muslim Traditions.*

If only there were a way towards union,
Or an army of patience in my heart.

'Erâqi

Patience is the stabilizing of the *nafs* in affliction;
And no matter what hardship the *nafs* incurs,
we would not let it flee from it.
If the *nafs* were made to moan a thousand times,
We would declare that this was a godsend.

Dâ'i Shirazi

'Patience' is said to symbolise tranquillity of heart throughout the suffering and hardship which the seeker undergoes on the path.

Let us maintain patience, to see
what her cruelty can do,
And what sadness for her would do
to this broken heart.

TT 211

'Patience' in the early stages signifies restraining the *nafs* from sinning, maintaining devotional practice through conviction, and refraining from complaint before anything other than God. In the final stages, 'patience' exists through God at the station of subsistence after annihilation.

RSh IV 174

Sahl ebn 'Abdo'llâh said, "Patience means maintaining patience within patience, that is to say, not being conscious of one's own patience; not wailing in affliction; and being aware that this power of patience is from God, Who has conferred it upon one, thereby enabling one to maintain it, as where He enjoins, "Have patience, for your patience is only through the help of God" (XVI: 127).

KST 284

The Sufis say that to commit oneself to patience involves the toleration of unpleasant things on the part of the *nafs*, and the tasting of bitterness. In other words, if one has not mastered patience, one must strive to be patient with total commitment. Patience is the abandonment of complaint before anything other than God.

Sahl said, "Patience means to await from God the release from difficulties; it is the noblest form and highest degree of service." Someone else has said that 'patience' is where "one compels oneself to be patient within patience." This means that one should not consider release, while one is in the state of 'patience'. In other words, one should not look forward to deliverance from afflictions and rigours while one is being subjected to them."

It has been said that 'patience' is where the devotee does not complain when affliction strikes, and 'contentment' is where the devotee is not disturbed when beset by affliction. Whatever is bestowed or taken away is by God's hand; who are you to be concerned?

Some say that 'patience' has three stations: The abandonment of complaint, which is the degree of the repentant; contentment with what is ordained, which is the degree of the ascetic; and loving-kindness, conferred by God, which is the degree of the sincere. These categories of 'patience' are maintained throughout calamity and affliction.

One should be aware that the nature of 'patience' varies according to the different degrees of canonical law to which it applies: 'Compulsory' or 'supererogatory', 'disapproved-of' or 'prohibited'. 'Patience' in restraint from what is 'prohibited' is 'compulsory' and in restraint from what is 'disapproved-of' is 'supererogatory'.

On the other hand, 'patience' in the face of that which torments one's consciousness is prohibited; for example, when one is tempted to commit a frobidden act because of a lustful thought and jealousy is provoked, one should maintain 'patience', restraining one's impulse to give vent to 'jealousy', and at the same time, observe patient restraint with respect to whatever is serving to tempt one into transgressions.

'Patience' with respect to that which is disapproved-of involves 'patience' in the face of torment over the temptation to do something which is disapproved of by canon law.

Thus, canon law must be the touchstone to determine the nature of patience.

KF 823

'Patience' is to abandon complaint about the pain of ordeal to other than God, as when God said of Job: "We found him patient"

(XXXVIII: 44), after Job had said, "Indeed, adversity has befallen me, and You are the Most Merciful of the Merciful" (XXI: 83).

Thus we see that if a devotee appeals to God to remove suffering and hardship, his 'patience' is not unacceptable.

TJ 88

THE DIFFERENCE BETWEEN PATIENCE AND AFFECTED PATIENCE *(farq bain-e ṣabr wa taṣabbor)*

'Patience' means the keeping of the *nafs* from things that are subject to disapproval, without anxiety and doubt.

'Affected patience' is the keeping of the *nafs* from things that are subject to disapproval, with anxiety and perturbation.

TKQ 591

DISTRESS *('enâ')*

'Distress' occurs in love in the early stages of devotion, in the course of rigorous austerities. Affliction occurs at the end of the station of love.

Hallâj said, "Distress brings ease to lovers and is the salt on the table of the loving ones."

MA 130

AFFLICTION *(balâ')*

'Affliction' represents the subjection of the gnostic to trial from God, so that in his devoteeship and in the eyes of God he does not neglect gnosis arising from love.

SS 573

'Affliction' is said to symbolise divine trial with a view to purifying the wayfarer in the course of his development.

Behind every affliction bestowed by God
  upon this group
There lies a treasure of blessings.

TT 178

'Affliction' signifies the probation of the bodies of the friends of God by various hardships, sicknesses, and sufferings. The more severe the affliction on the devotee, the nearer to God he becomes, for 'affliction' is the cloak of the friends of God, the foundation of the house of the pure, and the sustenance of the prophets.

The Prophet said, "For the prophets, affliction is more severe than for others."[1]

'Affliction' is a kind of suffering which affects the heart and body of the believer; its true nature is a blessing. The inner meaning of it, though, is hidden from the devotee so that he may withstand the pains thereof and gain divine recompense therefrom.

On the other hand, unbelievers are subjected not to 'affliction' but to 'misery' *(shaqâ')*, from which they receive no relief.

Subjection to 'affliction' is of a higher degree than that of 'trials' *(emteḥân)*, for the effect of 'trials' is upon the heart, while that of 'affliction' is upon both the heart and body.[2]

KM 504

'Affliction' signifies the devotee's being subject to ordeal from God in the reality of his state; this is the torment of God which descends on the devotee.

Abu Moḥammad Jorairi said, 'The human being is continuously subject to affliction."

LT 353

The 'affliction' of the lover arises from his Beloved being veiled from him for a time. Love itself is an 'affliction' which arises from the assault upon the spirit by the majestic theophany of God's grandeur and splendour. The lover's 'affliction' occurs only at the station where he is selected by God, as is alluded to by the Prophet when he said, "The severest affliction is reserved for the prophets."

The gnostic said, "Affliction is the beginning of stability and spiritual leadership *(imâmat)*. This is the meaning of the Koranic passage concerning God's desire to appoint Abraham the spiritual leader *(imâm)* of the worlds: "And when his Lord afflicted [tried] Abraham with His commands, and he fulfilled them, He said,

1. Cf. Foruzânfar *Aḥadith-e Mathnawi,* no. 30.
2. Nicholson's translation with minor changes, p. 388-89.

'Indeed, I have apointed you spiritual leader amongst mankind' " (II: 24).

MA 129

The ups and downs of the desert of love
comprise the snare of affliction;
Is there one so lion-hearted
as not to avoid affliction?

Ḥâfeẓ

Once again the heart has become
distant from your door;
Subjected to a hundred afflictions,
it has mastered patience.

'Erâqi

Shebli said, "Others love you for your blessings while I love you for your afflictions."

TS(S) 348

INJUSTICE *(jaur)*

'Injustice' is said to represent the blocking of the wayfarer from advancement in his spiritual ascent.[1]

EE 56

'Injustice' is said to symbolise the blocking of the wayfarer from 'witnessing' and from ascending to the high levels to which he aspires.

TT 188

Bear her injustice and seek no fidelity;
Bear her pain and seek no healing drug.

'Aṭṭâr

1. Cf. KF 296

What heart has not been brought to exasperation
    by your injustice?
What soul has not been brought to lamentation
    by your torment?

'Erâqi

COMPLAINT *(shekâyat)*

'Complaint' has three aspects: the first, 'complaint' about the Beloved to what is other than the Beloved, which results in dissaffection from the Beloved. The second is 'complaint' about what is other than the Beloved; this is infidelity with respect to the Beloved's loving-kindness. The third is 'complaint' about the Beloved to the Beloved; this is the essence of divine unity and detachment from self.

RSh I 198

O heart, do not complain, for I do not want
    my Beloved to hear you;
O heart, are you not afraid of my crying,
    "O Lord!" so much?

Rumi

Let me complain to the angels of mercy
    about the sadness from you,
For the physician has murdered me
    and refused to come to my grave!

Kamâl Khojandi

HAUGHTINESS *(takabbor)*

'Haughtiness' represents God's lack of need for any action on the part of the wayfarer.

EE58

'Haughtiness' is said to symbolise God's lack of need for anything in all the creation.

TT 184

SELF-SUFFICIENCY *(esteghnâ')*

'Self-sufficiency' connotes the possession of such wealth that the possessor has neither need for anything nor attachment to anything. The Sufis employ it in two different contexts. One is to represent the station attained by perfect gnostics in which there is an absence of need for anything but God. The other is to represent the station of Almighty Greatness *(kebriyâ)* and the divine absence of need before which the actions and efforts of the creatures of the world, even man's devotional and spiritual practices, are worthless.

Bring on the wine, for there is no distinction
in the court of self-sufficiency, whether
One be watchman or sultan, sober or drunk.

Ḥâfeẓ

In the *Manṭeq aṭ-ṭair (Conference of the Birds)*, 'Aṭṭâr considers 'self-sufficiency' to be the fourth of his seven valleys, coming between those of 'gnosis' and 'divine unity'.

REPUTATION *(âb-e-ru'i)*

Amongst the wayfarers of the path, 'reputation' is said to signify the inspiration from the unseen which infuses the hearts of wayfarers.

KF 1550

Come to us, seeking reputation
Come and abide in this infinite sea.

Shâh Ne'mato'llâh

DISGRACE *(roswâ'i)*

'Disgrace' is said to symbolise the stealing of the heart that occurs with the appearance of theophany, in such a way that the gnostic is left unaware of his outward condition.

TT 200-201

Love must be taken unveiled at the crossroads of disgrace.

'Aṭṭâr

O heart, be fair! With your wretchedness and disgrace,
how can you be worthy of love?

Rumi

JEALOUSY *(ghairat)*

'Jealousy' signifies the Sufi's zeal in his claim of love for God, for he does not want anyone to be closer to God than himself. This characteristic is particular to the novice wayfarer.

In Sufi terminology, 'jealousy' is of two kinds: that on the part of the Beloved and that on the part of the lover.

The Beloved's 'jealousy' is His jealousy with respect to His friends, insuring that they love no one but Him.

The lover's 'jealousy' is towards anyone who loves the Beloved more than he does.

Love's jealousy cut the tongues
of the elect ones,
Demanding why the secret of sadness for her
fell into the mouths of everyone.

Ḥâfeẓ

If it were not for the jealousy of your face,
O igniter of all fires,
The sun would not have drawn its dagger
across all horizons.

'Aṭṭâr

'Jealousy' represents the lover's zeal in seeking to cut off the regard which the Beloved has for others, and that of others towards the Beloved. It is one of the preconditions for 'loving-kindness'.

NFO 169

In the *Farhang-e Mo'in* God's 'jealousy' is defined as either that which prevents one from overstepping the limits of the path, or that which conceals mysteries and secrets. It may also signify God's protectiveness towards His friends.

'Jealousy' represents God's disapproval of the participation of what is other than Him in that which belongs to Him. (That is to say, since God is other than all existent beings, He does not want anyone to enjoy familiarity with anything other than Himself.)

TJ 109

The King is jealous of those who,
having seen the face, still follow other scents.
If God's jealousy is likened to a grain of wheat,
people's jealousy is the straw that's in the stack.
Know that the root of all jealousy is God;
that of created beings is unquestionably a branch thereof.

MM I 1770-1773

With God's jealousy, there is no recourse;
What heart has not been smashed into a hundred pieces by God's love?
Jealousy is this: he is other than all,
And he surpasses explanation and rhetorical clamour.

MM 1712-3

The whole world has become jealous with God,
Because he has preceded it in jealousy.
Since he is the soul and the world like a body,
That body accepts good and bad alike from the soul.

MM I 1763-4

In the early stages 'jealousy' opposes inclination towards and intimacy with what is other than the Beloved and slackening in one's pursuit of the path. In the final stages, it opposes the very existence of anything other than God.

RSh IV 178

Abu 'Othmân Maghrebi said, "Jealousy is an attribute of disciples and not of men of truth."

TA 785

Once when Râbe'a was sick, she was asked the cause of her

illness. She replied, "I looked at heaven once and I was chastised. It is His command that matters."

RQ 423

NON-FULFILLMENT *(nâ-morâdi)*[1]

'Non-fulfillment' is said to signify the heart's disinclination and aversion to sensual pleasures and the turning towards spiritual delight.

With all my heart
    I chose non-fulfillment with the world,
Because that is what you wanted
    of weary-hearted me.

TT 232

WAGERING-ALL-AWAY *(pâk-bâzi)*[2]

'Wagering-all-away' is said to represent pure intention in the performance of actions where one has no expectation of gaining merit or high status, but strives purely for God.

EE 72

'Wagering-all-away' is said to symbolise an intention which is pure of selfish instincts whether internal or external.

In the gambling-house of those *rendân*[3]
    who have wagered all away,
Forfeit all you have, in observing prayers or not.

TT 180-81

I went to the gambling-house
    and saw only those who had wagered all away;
I went to the cloister,
    and saw only pious hypocrites.

'Erâqi

1. Lit. 'desireless-ness'.
2. Lit. 'pure-losing'.
3. Plural of *rend,* see footnote p. 33.

Not only in this town did Sa'di become unequalled
For his wagering-all-away and being a *rend,*
but in every town around.

Sa'di

HASTE *(shetâb)*

'Haste' is said to represent the speed of journeying without consciousness of the gnosis of the nuances of stations. Such passage may be caused by attraction or through the wayfarer's effort in the form of actions, austerities, devotions, and purgation.

EE 72

The wine is in the pitcher and the lovers are drunk;
Do not languish, hasten and come!

Shâh Ne'mato'llâh

SLUGGISHNESS *(kâheli)*

'Sluggishness' is said to represent slowness of journeying, which may be due to the wayfarer's knowledge of the path, indicating his perfection, in which case it is the most perfect of passages, or it may be due to the wayfarer's faults, resulting in his lack of progress on the path, in which case it represents the least advanced of passages.

EE 71

You are sluggish because you are busy
enslaving the zephyr[1] every moment
With the scent of your tresses.

Ḥâfeẓ

It would be better if you put aside your sluggishness
In order to overtake your friends.

Rumi

1. *Bâd Sabâ*, see *Farhang-e Nurbakhsh*, Vol. II, p.36.

RELEASE *(faraj)*

'Release' symbolises the wayfarer's emergence from the bonds of human nature.

TT 219

O heart! Become engaged in sadness for him,
and be patient until he cures you,
For patience is the key to release.

Rumi

GIFT *(hadiya)*

The 'gift' is said to represent prophecy and friendship with God or any kind of divine selection or appointment.

EE 69

God's gift to the devotee is his soul, and the devotee's gift to God is the return of his soul to God, adorned, so that it might attract God's loving-kindness.

According to the Koran, Moḥammad said, "Follow me, that God may love you" (III: 31).

FM II 180

I am not asking for a gift from you, but only that you
become worthy of receiving a gift.

For I have rare gifts from the unseen that are beyond
human conception.

Rumi

SHARE *(naṣib)*

In Sufi terminology, whatever the *nafs* desires, or whatever accords with its desires is referred to as one's 'share'.

Esferâyeni wrote concerning the relation between 'the share' and pain and seeking, "Seeking should be such that it appears from within, its precondition being the heart's purity from any concern for one's 'share'. Whatever stems from the *nafs* and accords with the passions in either world is one's 'share'. The Prophet said, "For the person who awakes in the morning and finds that all his cares are one, God will relieve his cares in this world and the hereafter." That is to say, one should give up bargaining with God. Once one has abandoned any thought of having one's 'share', one's seeking becomes free of conditions. This freedom is the precondition for bondsmanship, and few attain to it. The true nature of this freedom is the abandonment of self. Whatever the wayfarers may perceive as their goal is not free from the sense of 'share', for that is their sole attachment.

MES 7

It is the sinners
who are worthy of generosity;
So go away O gnostic of God;
For heaven is our share!

Ḥâfeẓ

LOAN *(wâm)*

The 'loan' is said to represent unsolicited ordainment from God.

EE 63

Your beautiful eye has loaned
All its drunken mannerisms
to the narcissus.

Ḥâfeẓ

It's amazing that my hands are clean of both worlds;
yet in spite of this,
My neck still bears the burden of the loan of love.

Sanâ'i

SELF-SACRIFICING ONE *(fedâ'i)*

In the terminology of the lovers, the 'self-sacrificing one' is said to symbolise the lover who is ready to sacrifice his soul before his

 Beloved, as the moth sacrifices itself to the candle.

KF 1157

The self-sacrificing one will not give up his goal,
Even if he is showered with stones and arrows.

Sa'di

DISCUSSION *(goft-o gu'i)*

'Discussion' is said to represent loving reproach.

EE 72

Do you not remember her discussion that day?
She said, "Don't even think of my rose garden again!"

Rumi

Whatever you have heard from me you have heard
    from God;
For every discussion of mine is discussion from him.

Rumi

SEARCHING *(jost-o ju'i)*

'Searching' is said to represent fault-finding on the part of either lover or Beloved.

EE 72

I've thrown up my hands and given up searching;
My searching has died in the face of your searching.

Rumi

The heart became serene
    when it embraced the soul serene;
When the soul beheld
    the Soul of Souls, it rested from searching.

Maghrebi

'Searching' is said to represent fault-finding, whether on the part of the lover or that of the Beloved, which arises from the perfection of the relationship and unity which exists between them. Ḥâfeẓ writes:

O misery! O pain! In searching for the treasure
of the presence,
I begged and begged from the noble-hearted,
and nothing happened.

TT 187

Through discussion, the discourse of love
cannot be spoken;
Through searching, one cannot find union
with the companion.

'Erâqi

ATTRACTION AND EFFORT *(keshesh-o kushesh)*

'Attraction' signifies the Beloved's favour and encouragement towards the lover, while 'effort' is said to represent the lover's endeavour to attain the Beloved.

One must take a few steps in the way of 'effort' in order to attain the station of 'attraction'. "And those who strive in Us, indeed, We surely guide in Our paths" (XXIX: 69).

MES 10

Abu Sa'id Abe'l-Khair said that 'attraction' is better than 'effort', for unless there is attraction, there is no effort, and without effort there is no insight.

AT 307

I'm counting on the tip of your tresses
to be merciful.
What is the point of effort,
if from that tip there is no attraction?

Ḥâfeẓ

SINKING *(foru-raftan)*

'Sinking' is said to symbolise the immersion of the wayfarer in the contemplation of divine effects, acts, and attributes.

TT 220

Do not pass over like the writing pen;
Sink like ink into every world of His!

Kamâl Khojandi

GOING *(raftan)*

'Going' is said to represent ascent from the realm of human nature to that of the spirits.

EE 64

We have released the soul to the Soul of Souls,
and gone;
Who has done what we have done
and gone?

Rumi

When the heart recovered its calmness,
it did not remain
A moment with me in calmness;
it simply went.

'Erâqi

PASSING *(dhahâb)*

'Passing' signifies that which is more complete than 'absence', namely, the 'passing' of the heart from awareness of the objects of the senses to the witnessing of the unseen.[1]

LT 347

Whenever the gnostic becomes annihilated and enjoys his annihilation through the perception of the light of grandeur, he is called the 'one passing in annihilation'. This signifies the gnostic's

1. Cf. SS 566.

final stage of states, and his initial stage of stations.

Ḥallâj said, "Passing is the annihilation of existence in the Eternal Existent."

MA 200

PASSING OF PASSING *(dhahâb-e dhahâb)*

The 'passing of passing' signifies the absence of awareness of annihilation, that is to say, 'annihilation from annihilation'.

SS 566

The 'passing of passing' signifies the 'passing' from awareness of 'passing', which leads to annihilation from pleasure in one's awareness of Oneness *(aḥadiyat)*. When the wayfarer has become annihilated from all pleasure in unity, he arrives at the station of the 'passing of passing'.

Ḥallâj said, 'The passing of passing is absence from all that can be perceived of God's attributes and essence.

MA 200

SELLING *(forukhtan)*

'Selling' is said to represent the abandonment of the search for personal solutions and effort, before God.

EE 63

Although the friend will not
    buy us for anything,
We would not sell a strand
    of her hair for all the world.

Ḥâfeẓ

PAWNING *(gerau kardan)*

'Pawning' signifies the submission of one's being to divine ordainment and the abandoning of personal solutions and effort through one's own volition.

EE 63

In all temples of the Magi, there is no
love-crazed one like me,
Who has pawned, for wine, his cloak in one place
and his notebooks in another.

Ḥâfeẓ

EXCHANGING *(badal kardan)*

'Exchanging' is said to represent the diversion of inclination from one thing to another for a given reason.

EE 64

FORFEITING *(dar bâkhtan)*

'Forfeiting' is said to represent the obliteration of past actions from the inner being.

EE 64

'Forfeiting' is said to signify the obliteration of previous actions which have assumed importance to the wayfarer.

TT 195

The lover forfeited his soul many times
for that face in the way of love.
He became a clean losing gambler,
having lost so many times.

Kamâl Khojandi

LOSING *(bâkhtan)*

'Losing' is said to symbolise the turning of the heart away from the forms of essences *(a'yân).*

However much you have won or lost,
You throw it all into running water.

TT 175

When your lips play the game of allurement
I lose my soul to you;
Whatever is to be lost
must be lost to one's opponent.

Kamâl Khojandi

IMPLORING *(lâba kardan)*

'Imploring' is said to represent the overwhelming of the wayfarer by the power and dominion of love.

In response to my imploring she declared, "One night,
I shall be the honoured guest at your assembly;"
As she desired, I became her abject slave;
yet still she did not come.

Ḥâfez

Because all my imploring and complaining
reached the heavens,
Gabriel and the heavenly host
look after only me in the world.

Rumi

ABANDONING *(tark kardan)*

'Abandoning' is said to signify the severance of expectation in something.

EE 64

I will not abandon love
and witness and goblet;
A hundred times have I repented;
I'll not do it again.

Ḥâfeẓ

RISING *(bar khâstan)*

'Rising' is said to represent the wayfarer's purpose and resolve.

EE 64

'Rising' symbolises sincere resolve which is focused on the Source of Unity in such a way as to cause both inward and outward attachments to be severed.

TT 177-178

I'm the moth of the Beloved; I burn and I endure.
Drunken and delirious, I fall and I rise.

Rumi

Let me rise and lay my head at your feet;
Let me sit and sacrifice my soul for you.

Bibi Ḥayâti

As the vat of wine began to flow
from the winehouse,
One hundred souls rose before it.

'Erâqi

SITTING *(neshastan)*

'Sitting' is said to represent tranquillity.

EE 64

'Sitting' is said to symbolise the calmness and serenity of the heart from dispersive thoughts and disturbed preoccupations in the course of journeying towards God and with God.

TT 232

Having shaken the two worlds from his sleeve,
He sits in the winehouse like a *qalandar*.[1]

'Erâqi

1. The term *qalandar* refers to a person whose outward appearance and behaviour does not conform to the dogmatic requirements of a particular religion, but whose heart and inner feelings are directed towards God. See also *Farhang-e Nurbakhsh*, Vol. VI, p. 167.

You cannot sit with illumined heart
    until you have burned all that you possess;
First the moth must be consumed,
    then it may sit with the candle.

Kamâl Khojandi

Without heart and a sweetheart, I cannot sit;
Without the beauty of the companion, I cannot sit.

Maghrebi

O you who have broken my repentance,
    where can I flee from you?
O you who sit in my heart,
    where can I flee from you?

Rumi

COMING *(âmadan)*

'Coming' is said to represent return to the realm of human nature from the realm of the spirit, or the realm of immersion or the realm of intoxication.

EE 64

'Coming' is said to symbolise the return of the gnostic in union from the expanse of the realm of Lordship to the station of human nature and the level of outward form.

TT 172

How happy the time
    when the beloved came,
For he is the consoler,
    coming to comfort the sad ones.

Ḥâfeẓ

I've come again like the new year,
to break the lock on the prison,
To smash the teeth and shatter the claws
of this man-eating world.

Rumi

REMEMBERING *(yâd âvordan)*

'Remembering' signifies the compound perception which results from innate gnosis and the antecedence of pre-eternal acquaintanceship, "Indeed, therein is truly a reminder for those of understanding" (XXXIX: 21). Shabestâri illustrates this in the following line from his *Golshan-e râz:*

Know that the word of God has descended,
That you might remember that primal pledge.

TT 237

Remember those mighty conversations
I had with your tresses,
Talking of the mystery of love
and reaching the circle of the lovers?

Ḥâfeẓ

REPOSING *(ghonudan)*

'Reposing' is said to signify the veiling of the light of insight from the witnessing of the nuances of the creation, as well as obliviousness to the mysteries of the spiritual realm.

TT 219

O my heart, if a heart should emit such wails
on the night of separation,
I hope that no one would even dream of you in repose.

Kamâl Khojandi

BURNING *(suzândan)*

In sufi terminology 'burning' signifies the intermediate stages of theophanies which attract the wayfarer towards annihilation, the first stages being 'lightning' *(barq)* and the last being 'obliteration in the Essence'.

TJ 59

If I were to fly a hair's-breadth higher,
The brilliance of theophany
would burn my feathers[1]

Sa'di

BEING BURNED UP, CONSUMED *(sukhtan)*[2]

As the lights of the splendour and the grandeur of God appear and encompass the spirit of the yearning one, his inner consciousness is burned in the lights of the majesty, such that he is consumed by God, in God, for God.

The gnostic said, "To be burned up signifies the liberation of the inner consciousness through love, from all that is other than God."

MA 113

One may be consumed in one of two ways, either in fire or by means of light. Whoever is consumed by fire becomes ash and has no value, while whoever is consumed by light becomes a lamp which gives benefit to all.

TKQ 733

Abo'l-Ḥasan Kharaqâni said, "The first step is to submit to God and nothing else; the second is to be intimate; and the third is to be burned up."

TA 706

Although Ḥâfeẓ has been burned up, he still
remains faithful to his pledge
As the condition of love and soul-sacrifice.

Ḥâfeẓ

1. Legend has it that these words were spoken to Moḥammad by Gabriel during Mohammad's nocturnal journey *(me'râj)*. Cf. Schimmel, *And Moḥammad is His Messenger* (Chapel Hill: 1985) p. 169, and Nicholson R.A., *Mathnawi of Jalâlu'ddin Rumi,* Books I & II commentary (Cambridge: 1937) I: 1066.

2. *Al-eḥterâq.*

The 'pledge' is one of the stations of the sincere.

When God summoned the host of the spirits of lovers to the court of vision, he revealed himself to them in the form of utterance, asking, "Am I not your Lord?" (VII: 172). In reply, the lovers bore witness to his Lordship; God then made a 'pledge' of love to them, having them testify to the pledge by stating that they would choose nothing over him.

After they had become separated from the realm of the unseen and had entered the corporeal realm, they looked upon the creatures therein and sought the creator of those creatures, in order to return to God, not being content with anything other than God. Accordingly, they became re-united with their origin through intense yearning and love, and disaffected by that which was other than God, for they had been created as spirits from the angelic realm, and founded repose only in the source of sanctity and the garden of intimacy. The Koran refers to "...men who are true to what they have covenanted with God" (XXXIII: 23) and to "...those who keep their pledge when they make one..." (II: 177).

The Prophet said, "The virtuous pledge comes through sincere faith." The pledge of the gnostic is made only at the station of devotion, where the *nafs* is striving; when the gnostic attains the station of stability, he abandons the pledge, for it is made to the pre-eternal ordainment of God; at the station of the sincerity of trust-in-God *(tawakkol),* there is no pledge because every pledge made by the gnostic is broken at the station of love.

'Ali said, "I have known God through breaking resolutions and abolishing cares." A Sufi master has said, "It is thirty years since I gave up making pledges and I make no compacts for fear that I shall break them."

The gnostic said, "The pledge binds the inner consciousness with adherence to sincerity in loving-kindness."

MA 73

Though sadness for you has blown away
  the harvest of my life,
I swear upon the dust beneath your feet,
  I did not break my pledge!

Ḥâfeẓ

The 'covenant', ('divine pledge' or 'pre-eternal pledge') is the covenant made between God and his devotees in pre-eternity, to which the Koranic verse known as the 'Verse of the Covenant' refers, "And when your Lord summoned the children of Adam and their descendants from their loins, and made them bear witness on themselves, asking, 'Am I not your Lord?' they said, 'Yes, we bear witness' " (VII: 172).

From the crack of the dawn of pre-eternity
to the end of the evening of post-eternity,
Friendship and affection have been based upon
one pledge and one covenant.

Ḥâfeẓ

The 'covenant' is one of the stations of the sincere.

Whenever God desires to intensify gnosis, bringing the gnostic to realisation in loving-kindness, He calls him to Himself through union and nearness and places the gnostic in the seat of dominion, addressing him as if he were a noble one. God commands the gnostic to perform great things in servanthood and binds him to the 'covenant' of Lordship. The terms of the covenant are the gnostic's veneration and reverence for God's ordainment and that the gnostic must never become separated from gnosis by becoming engaged in the pleasures of the *nafs* while following Satan, despite his involvement in the veil of the world.

This 'covenant' is a tradition which was originaly established between God and the great prophets and friends of God, as referred to in such verses as, "When God made a covenant with the prophets..." (III: 81).

The gnostic said, "The covenant from God represents the opening of the doors of expansion with the key of dignity, while the the gnostic's covenant represents the offering up of his spirit through surrender."

MA 74

The 'Verse of the Covenant' (VII: 172) holds a vital place in Sufi thought. Jonaid founded his theory and practice of Sufism upon it.

For Jonaid, the 'Verse of the Covenant' provided a manifest proof, that the existence of humanity is founded upon the human being existing only for his Lord, such that he does not exist with regard to that which is other than God. Jonaid's position is that the clearest way for the Sufi to traverse the path is by striving to return to the state prior to his coming into existence, in other words, the state of the 'covenant'.

From the theoretical point of view, the 'covenant' is the principle by which the theories of annihilation, divine unity and Divinity *(oluhiyat)* are interpreted.

Ebn 'Arabi was fully aware of the importance of the 'Verse of the Covenant' in Sufi thought, and although he did not use it as the basis on which he built his own theory and practice of Sufism, he did accept it. Ebn 'Arabi's position was that the devotee's relationship with the 'covenant' is distinct from his relationship with Lordship. He maintained that the 'covenant' represents the very human nature with which a person is born, which he termed the '"yes"[1] nature' *(feṭrat-e bali)*.

al-Mo'jam aṣ-Ṣufi 1122

You ask me to tell you
about the secret of the pre-eternal pledge;
I will tell you when I have
downed two cups of wine.

Ḥâfeẓ

REGARD *(naẓar)*

'Regard' is employed in various contexts in Sufi poetry, several of which we present below.

In the sense of casting a 'look':

You tore the veil from your face
and cast a regard
Which caused the heavenly nymphs
to be veiled in shame.

Ḥâfeẓ

In the sense of a 'look' combined with insight and intuitive 'tasting' *(dhauq)*:

1. Koran: VII 172.

Someone who had insight in the science
    of regard said, "O Heart,
If you are a connoisseur of beauty,
    seek the mystery-of-beauty from the idols."

Ḥâfeẓ

Not every reed's a sugar-cane;
Not every low point has a high;
Not every eye has a regard,
Not every ocean has a pearl.

Rumi

'Regard' can also be used in the sense of a 'look' with attention and desire of heart, that is to say, a 'spiritual look', which is said to be particularly employed by the Sufis, as indicated by such expression as "So-and-so is under the Master's regard," or "O Master, grant me a regard!"

The following verse is a Sufi proverb:

Forty retreats! O forty retreats and forty
    retreats!
One regard from the master is better than forty retreats!

Rumi

O Beloved! By your blessed eyes
    give an allusion with your eye!
For a moment reinforce
    your devastated one with a regard!

Rumi

Scarcely had your eye
    cast its regard upon the monks
Than every monk within the cloister
    let out a drunken shout.

Kamâl Khojandi

'Regard' may also refer to the special attention from God which is focused on the wayfarer.

The heart is immersed in the lights
of the beauty and majesty;
The heart-ravisher's regard is constantly upon it.

Maghrebi

I am the slave of the aspiration
of one whose aspiration is mighty,
Who possesses both the worlds
and finds the heart with one regard.

Sanâ'i

Ḥallâj said, "Whoever gains regard [that is to say, vision of God] ceases to need news of God, and whoever attains the object of regard, ceases to need regard."

SS 471

'Regard' is sometimes used in conjunction with other terms, as in the expression 'amorous regard' *(naẓar-bâzi)*[1], which is applied in two contexts in Sufism: Firstly, it can be used in the sense of gazing at a beautiful face, where certain masters have considered the beauty of those so graced to be the reflection of the Divine Beauty. This has made them *'naẓar-baz'* or 'worshippers of beauty'.

Those who are unaware are
confounded by our amorous regard;
I am what I appear to be;
they may think whatever they wish.

Ḥâfeẓ

Secondly, it can be used in the sense of the exchange of glances between lover and Beloved:

1. Lit. regard play.

The perfection of charm and beauty
comes about in amorous regard;
Be the paragon of your time,
by the manner of your regard.

Ḥâfeẓ

KINDS OF REGARD *(anwâ'-e naẓar)*

'Regard' is of two kinds, the human and the divine. The human is where you regard yourself, while the Divine is where God regards you. As long as regard for yourself remains planted in your consciousness, God's regard for you will not enter your heart.

KAM VIII 57

The 'regard of the ordinary people' extends only as far as the Acts; the field of the 'regard of the elect' extends to the Attributes, and the site of the 'regard of the elect of the elect' is the majesty of the Essence.

KAM VI 529

ATTENTION *(tawajjoh)*

'Attention' means to look in one direction, inwardly and outwardly.

What is our attention?
It is to turn our face
from all but the friend.

Dâ'i Shirâzi

Perfect 'attention' to God is total inward and outward concentration on God in one's essence and in all of one's attributes, as well as the shedding of any motivation towards anything other than God, such that no beloved, aim, or desired one, remains but God.

RSh I 195

THE DIFFERENCE BETWEEN ATTENTION AND CAREFULNESS *(farq bain-e tawajjoh wa deqqat)*

Normally, 'attention' is associated with the senses, while 'carefulness' involves the intellect and knowledge. 'Carefulness' requires 'attention', whereas 'attention' does not require 'carefulness'.

GLANCE FROM THE CORNER OF THE EYE *(gusha-ye cheshm)*

The 'glance from the corner of the eye' signifies a darting look from the corner of the eye.

All my life I have fallen wretched in her way;
Out of coyness she withheld the glance
  from the corner of her eye.

Sabzawâri

Whoever does not avert his gaze
  from the glance from the corner of that eye
Is a bird who has no fear
  of being stalked by the hunter.

Kamâl Khojandi

GLANCE AND GLIMPSE *(laḥẓ wa laḥẓa)*

A 'glance' connotes the scanning of an object with the eyes or looking at it from the corner of the eye.

A 'glimpse' is a look from the corner of the eye; the word *laḥẓa* means an 'instant' or 'twinkling of an eye'.

So, at every instant you undergo
  dying and returning;
The Prophet said that the world
  is no more than an hour.

MM I 1142

The 'glance' is an allusion to the eye of the heart contemplating that which has become apparent because of certitude. The true nature of 'glancing' is the inner conciousness seeing itself as non-being looking at all-being and as God looking to God in the course of the vision of the beauty of the Beauty. This is duality from the point of view of the divine unity.

SS 575

The 'glance' is said to represent the attention of the eye of the heart on that which appears because of certainty. This certitude is a result of belief in the unseen.

LT 355

The 'glance' is one of the stations of the visionaries*(shâhed)*.

When the inner consciousness of the gnostic, in the course of his journey, becomes purged of the taint of the heart's witnessing of that which is other than the Lord, his heart longs overwhelmingly to perceive the beauty of witnessing in the sky of certitude. Then he comes to seek God unquestioningly, bewildered by the loss of his beloved. Thereupon the Beauty of the Eternal suddenly becomes revealed to him; he becomes frightened and unable to bear the sight of it, having reached the limit of endurance in his witnessing. At this point, he comes to observe it with glimpses of his inner consciousness, receiving draughts from the chalices of the seas of yearning, loving-kindness, and intimacy.

God said to Moḥammad, when he was at this station: "We have seen your face turn towards the heavens" (II: 144). In describing the flight of Moḥammad's spirit, while prostrating during meditation with the angels, the Koran says that "he approached and descended..." (LIII: 8) and speaks of God, "Who sees you when you stand to pray and sees your abasement among those who fall prostrate in worship" (XXVI: 218-9).

The gnostic said, "Glancing refers to the speed with which the eye of the inner consciousness instantaneously catches the light of God at the site of the vision of nearness."

MA 157

God said to Moses, "Look at the mountain, if it remains firm in its place, then will you see Me" (VII: 143).

'Glancing' lasts only an instant and has three degrees. The first is to observe the antecedent grace of God. This blocks any appeal, except as an expression of the abjectness which is worthy of Lordship. This cultivates and fosters joy unless it is tempered with wariness of

God's deception *(makr)* and motivates gratitude unless God expresses that gratitude Himself.

The second is the observation of the light of visionary revelation, which unveils friendship, stimulates the taste for theophany, and preserves one from the shame of unwarranted consolation.

The third is the observation of the essence of concentration *(jam')* which serves as a stimulus for one to consider the inadequacy of one's efforts. It grants liberation from the foolishness of one's opposition to God and brings benefit through contemplation in the early stages of the path.

MS 170

The ninetieth field is that of the glimpse, which follows that of ecstacy.

God said to Moses, "Look at the mountain, if it remains firm in its place, then will you see Me" (VII: 143).

The 'glimpsing of the ecstatic' occurs when the inward eye falls upon an object of the heart's desire. Those who experience this are of three types.

The first is the 'awestruck one', who seeks that object, is deceived [by God], and is then slain in order to become close [to God].

The second is the 'lover', who seeks the Friend, sees a sign and then becomes detached from everything in order to become close.

The third is the 'intimate one', who observes the moment, sees the light, and then becomes drowned in order to become close.

The first becomes engaged in service and asceticism; the second arrives at respect and modesty; and the last remains separate from himself and becomes liberated.

SM 331

Rowaim said, "'Glimpsing' brings ease, an inspiration arouses action, and 'allusions' *(eshâra)* bring good tidings."

TA 486

Shebli said, "'Glimpsing' is bereavement, inspiration is disappointment, 'allusion' is estrangement, and 'miracles' are alibis.

TA 636

An 'allusion' signifies an intimation by nod or gesture.

Shebli said, "One who makes an allusion towards God is no more than an idolator, for allusion is appropriate only towards idols."

LT 337

'Allusion' signifies an enigmatic utterance without explanation.

KM 500

'Allusion' is polytheism with respect to unity, for it designates delimitation [unity being limitless]. It is a kind of divine disguise, since it issues from the source of separative consciousness and thence proceeds to the source of divine unity.

SS 561

When the visionary is at the intermediate stage of the path and the light of nearness prevails over his heart, an 'allusion' of God appears in every instance of motion and rest which infuses his inner consciousness. This 'allusion' arises from an excess of loving-kindness, not from gratitude, and, as a result of this, his inner consciousness dominates his whole body. When he receives a command [from God] his whole being immediately responds in his 'allusion' of God. The visionary comprehends this state because 'allusion' is an instantaneous state of jealousy and is pardonable at the station of gnosis and divine unity.

Note how Zachariah held his tongue because of the mystery of his state and made 'allusion' (IX: 3). The Koran also tells how the Lord "inspired them" (XIV: 13), that is to say, 'gave them allusion'.

'Allusion' involves the gesture of the limb. Jonaid recounted, "I was sitting with Ebn Karbâni, I indicated with my head towards the heavens. He said, 'That is distance.' Then I indicated towards the earth. Still he said, 'That is distance.' Ebn Karbâni rejected 'allusion' because he was at the station of divine unity."

The gnostic said, "Allusion is the gesturing of the inner consciousness towards the light, of the light towards the unseen, and of the unseen towards the pre-eternal source."

MA 164

'Allusion' means to inform someone else of the object of one's desire without stating it directly.

KM 500

When loving-kindness overwhelms the heart of the visionary, he becomes established in intimacy [with God], enjoying vision of God in every particle. When he wishes to communicate something of the mystery of his vision, he gives an 'allusion' to it by some description or by naming an action or attribute [of God]. The visionary is, so to speak, 'present in the very absence' and 'absent in the very presence', where most of his words become vehicles of 'allusions' such as 'the One Who' and pronouns like 'He'.

It may appear that the visionary has perceived what he has seen and is trying to conceal it, whereas he has no other means of communicating the subtlety of what he has seen except through 'allusion'.

From the point of view of divine unity, 'allusion' is unbelief, while from the point of view of love, 'allusion' is in accordance with divine unity.

God in his sanctity and transcendence describes himself in the following terms: "Blessed is He..." (LXVII: 1), and "And He is the All-hearing, the All-seeing" (XLII: 11).

Shebli said, "Any allusion by which a created being refers to God refers back to himself, unless he is alluding through God to God, in which case the created being is not responsible for this allusion."

The gnostic said, "Allusion' is the 'divine right' of love, for love sees nothing but God. Love's allusion is 'absence' with respect to created being and 'presence' with respect to God."

MA 163-64

'Allusion' signifies that which exists in its own right but has not been referred to directly.

TJ 17

When Abu 'Ali Rudbâri was asked about 'allusion', he said, "Allusion is the concealing of information concerning a person which has been received directly from that person and not through a third party. 'Allusion' must be based on reasons but reasons are far from truths."

TS(S) 364

'Allusion' is that which is difficult to express directly because of the subtlety of its meaning. Rudbâri said, "Our knowledge is 'allusion', and if it were ever stated directly, it could not be comprehended." The true nature of 'allusion' is the sparkling *(lama'at)* of the light of subtle and inwardly realised utterance from God, clothed in mystery and accompanied by the onrush of total ecstasy within the heart. The gnostic alludes to this with the tongue of Divine Reality from the source of union, to the people of God, in order to intimate thereby something of visionary revelation in the course of the expansion of the spirit, the spirit being present, witnessing and speaking truly from God.

LT 337

The one who receives good tidings
    is one who understands allusion.
There are many subtle points,
    but where is the one privy to the secrets?

Ḥâfeẓ

Shahriyâr Kâzeruni said, "The pleasure of the *nafs* is to voice expressions, while allusion is the pleasure of the spirit. Expression belongs to the body, allusion to the spirit."

TA 773

Abo'l-Ḥasan Nuri said, "Allusion requires no words and to be capable of allusion to God the inner conciousness must be drowned in sincerity."

TA 473

Shebli said, "Expression is the tongue of knowledge, while allusion is the tongue of gnosis."

TA 632

I am reeling so much
from drunkenness and devastation,
That I cannot distinguish
a statement from an allusion.

Sanâ'i

Abo'l-Qâsem Naṣrâbâdi said, "Allusion arises from the incapacity and selfishness of human nature which cannot conceal a secret, and expresses it therefore through 'allusion'.

TA 793

Jonaid of Baghdad said, 'Aspiration' *(hemmat)* is God's allusion; devotion is that of the angels; inspiration that of gnosis; adornment that of the body; passions that of the *nafs* and self-indulgence that of unbelief."

TA 440

THE ALLUDER *(ṣâḥeb-e eshâra)*

The 'alluder' is someone whose speech embraces subtleties, allusions, and the science of gnosis.

LT 360

METAPHOR*(kenâya)*

'Metaphor' and 'allusion' *(eshâra)* are similar to one another. 'Metaphor' is clearer than allusion inasmuch as it brings news of God to the seekers of the unseen through the tongue of expansion. At times, 'metaphor' refers to a name for a thing by a name by which it is not usually known so that the visionary may perceive it, while the one who is absent is none the wiser.

The gnostic experiences 'metaphor' through vision at the station of mysteries and expansion. 'Metaphor' is employed in the Koran, as in the verse, "And they both ate earthly food"[1] (V: 75).

1. The reference is to Jesus and Mary and alludes to the fact that they were both ordinary human beings.

The gnostic said, "Metaphor concerns information about state, expressed cryptically, out of jealousy to protect the state."

MA 164

The breaths of Jesus are a subtle
reference to your lips;
Khedhr's water is a metaphor
for the life force given from your lips.

Ḥâfeẓ

SYMBOL *(ramz)*

'Symbol' is said to be the manifestation of divine secrets at the level of the inner consciousness through the devotions of the *nafs*, as well as allusions of the intellect. Ḥâfeẓ writes:

If I could but receive a symbol
of your beauty's traits,
I would not pay a penny
for all the maidens of paradise.

TT 201

'Symbol' represents the inward meaning of outward utterance, which brings realisation only to God's adherents. The true nature of symbol comprises the truths of the unseen in the nuances of knowledge, articulated enigmatically by the tongue of the inner consciousness.

SS 561

'Symbol' is the appearance of the light of inspiration in the heart of the visionary who enjoys presence at the time when the morning of certitude dawns and the light of witnessing is revealed; it is the time when the gnostic recognises, through divine inspiration, the wisdom of the truths of divine attributes and acts; it is proof of the unseen through which subtle expressions and angelic 'symbols' flow to his inner consciousness and fall from his lips, or when he experiences gnosis. This is an 'allegory', in which is hidden gnosis of the reality of religion, which can be gleaned only by gnostics of God.

In the Koran we note that God's prophet Zachariah, who when

his heart was involved in the vision of the unseen and his tongue was prevented from disclosing the secrets of the mysteries, was instructed, "You shall not speak with people for three days except through signs" (III: 41).

Abu Naṣr Sarrâj said, "The symbol is a spiritual reality disguised in outward utterance, being evident only to those who are privy thereto."

The gnostic said, "A symbol is the voice of the inner consciousness revealing what is cognised from the realm of the unseen, through the tongue of cognition."

MA 165

Qannâd said, "When they speak, you are incapable of perceiving the meaning of their symbols; and when they are silent, it is impossible for you to comprehend their meaning." One master said, "Whoever wishes to understand the symbols of our masters must look into their personal letters and correspondence, for their symbols are found therein, not in their formal writings."

LT 338

BIBLIGORAPHY

Abu Sa'di Abe'l-Khair. *Asrâr at-tauhid.* See Monawwar.

Anṣâri, Khwâja 'Abdo'llâh. *Manâzel as-sâ'erin,* including *'Elal al-maqâmât. Sad maidân*, and sections of the *Tafsir*. Edited by S. Laugier de Beaurecueil. Persian trans., introduction and notes by Rawân Farhâdi. Kabul, 1976.

____. *Rasâ'el-e jâme'-e Khwâja 'Abdo'llâh-e Anṣâri.* Edited by Waḥid Dastgerdi. Tehran, 1968.

____. *Majmu'a-ye Rasâ'el-e Khwâja 'Abdo'llâh-e Anṣâri.* Edited by Moḥammad Shirwâni, Tehran, 1963.

____. *Ṭabaqât aṣ-ṣufiya.* Edited by 'Abdo'l-Ḥayy Ḥabibi. Kabul, 1968.

____. *Tafsir 'erfâni wa adabi-ye Qor'ân-e majid.* Edited by Ḥabibo'llâh Amuzagâr. Tehran, 1969.

Arberry, A.J., trans. *The Doctrine of the Sufis*. Partial translation of Kalâbâdhi's *Kitâb at-ta'arrof.* Cambridge University Press, 1977.

____. *The Koran Interpreted.* Oxford University Press, 1983.

____. trans. *Muslim Saints and Mystics.* Partial translation of 'Aṭṭâr's *Tadhkerat al-auliyâ'*. London, 1976.

'Aṭṭâr, Farido'd-Din. *Diwân-e qasâ'ed wa tarji'ât wa ghazaliyât.* Edited by Sa'id Nafisi. Tehran, 1960.

____. *Moṣibat-nâma.* Edited by Nurâni Wesâl. Tehran, 1977.

____. *Tadhkerat al-auliyâ'.* Edited by Moḥammad Este'lâmi. Tehran, 1975.

Bâbâ Tâher 'Oriyân, *Sharḥ-e aḥwâl wa âthâr wa do-baitihâ-ye Bâbâ Ṭâher.* Including the *Sharḥ wa tarjoma-ye kalamât-e qeṣâr* ascribed to 'Aino'l-Qoḍhât Hamadâni. Edited by Javâd Maqṣur. Tehran, 1975.

Bâkhrazi, Abo'l-Mofâkher. *Aurâd al-ahbâb wa foṣuṣ al-âdâb.* 2 Vols. Edited by Iraj Afshâr. Tehran, 1979.

Bertels, Yevgeni, Edvardovich. *Mer'ât-e 'oshshâq* (Persian), in *Tasawwof wa adabiyât-e tasawwof.* Translated from Russian into Persian by Sirus Izadi. Tehran, 1979.

Bibi Ḥayâti. See Kermâni.

Dâ'i Shirâzi, (Shâh Dâ'i- elâ'llâh) *Kolliyât-e Shâh Dâ'i Shirâzi.* Edited by Maḥmud Dabir Siyâqi. Tehran, 1961.

Dârâbi, Moḥammad *Latifa-ye ghaibi.* Nurbakhsh Library, Tehran, Photocopy, (n.d.).

Dehkhodâ, 'Ali Akbar. *Loghat-nâma.* Compiled under the supervision of Dr Moḥammad Mo'in. Tehran, 1947-73.

Ebn'al-'Arabi, Moḥyiyo'd-din. *Foṣuṣ al-hekam.* Edited by Abo'l-A'lâ 'Affifi. Beirut, 1980.

——. *Fotuḥât al-makkiya.* 4 Vols. Cairo, 1911.

'Erâqi, Fakhro'd-Din Ebrâhim. *Kolliyât-e 'Erâqi.* Edited by Sa'id Nafisi. Tehran, 1959.

——. *Resâla-ye lama'ât wa resâla-ye eṣṭelâḥât.* Edited by Javâd Nurbakhsh. Tehran, 1974.

Eṣfahâni, Hâtef. *Diwan.* Edited by Waḥiḍ Dastgerdi. Tehran, 1970.

Esfarâyeni, 'Abdo'r-Raḥmân. *Maktubât-e 'Abdo'r-Raḥmân-e Esfarâyeni ba A'lâ'o'd-Daula-ye Semnâni.* Edited by Herman Landolt. Tehran, Paris, 1972.

Foruzânfar, Badi'oz-Zamân. *Aḥâdith-e Mathnawi,* 3rd ed. Tehran, 1982.

Ḥâfeẓ, Shamso'd-Din Moḥammad. *Diwân.* Edited by Sayyed Abo'l-Qâsem Anjawi Shirâzi. Shiraz, 1982.

Hamadâni, 'Aino'l-Qoḍhât. *Resâla-ye lawâ'eḥ.* Edited by Raḥim Farmânesh. Tehran, 1958.

Hâtef Eṣfahâni. See Eṣfahâni, Hâtef.

Hojwiri, 'Ali ebn 'Othmân.*Kashf al-maḥjub.* Persian text edited by V.A. Zhukovsky. Leningrad, 1926.

Iraqi, Fakhruddin. *Divine Flashes.* Translated by W.C. Chittick and P.L. Wilson. London, 1982.

Jâmi, 'Abdo'r-Raḥmân. *Nafaḥât al-ons.* Edited by Mehdi Tauḥidipur. Tehran, 1964.

Jorjâni, 'Ali ebn Moḥammad. *At-Ta'rifât.* Edited by Gustavus Fleugel. Leipzig, 1845.

Kamâl Khojandi. See Khojandi.

Kalâbâdhi, Abu Bakr Moḥammad. *at-Ta'arrof le-madhhab ahl at-taṣawwof.* Persian translation by Abu Ebrâhim Mostamli, *Sharḥ-e Ta'arrof.* 4 Vols. Lucknow, 1912. The author has used a Persian commentary on the text *Kholâṣa-ye Sharḥ-e Ta'arrof.* Edited by Aḥmad 'Ali Rajâ'i. Tehran, 1970.

Kâshâni, 'Abdo'r-Razzâq. *Eṣṭelâḥât aṣ-ṣufya.* Edited by Moḥammad Kamâl Ebrâhim Ja'far. Egypt, 1984.

Kâshâni, 'Ezzo'd-Din Maḥmud. *Meṣbâh al-hedâya wa meftâh al-kefâya.* Edited by Jalâlo'd-Din Homâ'i. Tehran, 1946.

Kermâni, Bibi Ḥayâti. *Diwân-e Ḥayâti Kermâni.* Edited by Javad Nurbakhsh. Tehran, 1971.

Kharaqâni, Shaikh Abo'l-Ḥasan. *Aḥwâl wa aqwâl-e Shaikh Abo'l-Ḥasan-e Kharaqâni,* including *Montakhab-e nuro'l-'olum.* Edited by Mojtabâ Minowi. Tehran, 1980.

Khojandi, Kamâl. *Diwân-e Kamâlo'd-Din Mas'ud-e Khojandi.* Edited by 'Aziz Daulatâbâdi. Tehran, 1958.

Lâhiji, Shamso'd-Din Moḥammad, (Asiri). *Diwân-e ash'âr wa rasâ'el.* Edited by Barât Zanjâni. Tehran, 1978.

____. *Mafâtiḥ al-e'jâz fi sharḥ-e Golshan-e râz.* Edited by Kaiwân Sami'i. Tehran, 1958.

Maghrebi, Moḥammad Shirin. *Diwân-e kâmel-e Shams-e Maghrebi,* including *Resâla-ye jâm-e jahân-namâ.* Edited by Abu Ṭâleb 'Abedini. Tehran, 1979.

____. *Diwân-e Moḥammad Shirin Maghrebi.* Edited by Leonard Lewisohn. Forthcoming.

Mo'in, Moḥammad. *Farhang-e fârsi.* 6 Vols. Tehran, 1981.

Maibodi, Abo'l-Faḍhl Rashido'd-Din. *Kashf al-asrâr wa 'oddat al-asrâr.* 10 Vols. Edited by 'Ali-Asghar Ḥekmat. Tehran, 1978.

Monawwar, Moḥammad ebn al-. *Asrâr at-tauḥid fi maqâmât ash-Shaikh Abu Sa'id.* Edited by Ḍhabiho'llâh Ṣafâ. Tehran, 1928.

Nâṣer Khosrau Qobâdiyâni. *Diwân,* including *Roshanâ'i-nâma* and *Sa'âdat-nâma.* Edited by Mojtabâ Minowi. Tehran, 1928.

Ne'mato'llâh, Sayyed Nuro'd-Din. See Shâh Ne'mato'llâh.

Neẓâmi Ganjawi, (Ḥakim) Elyâs. *Kolliyât-e khamsa-ye Ḥakim Neẓâmi-ye Ganjawi.* Tehran, 1972.

Nicholson, R.A., trans. *Kashf al-maḥjub of al-Hujwiri.* E.J.W. Gibb memorial series Vol. XVII, 1911, reprint, London: Luzac, 1976.

____. trans., ed. *The Mathnawi of Jalâlu'ddin Rumi,* 4th ed., 3 Vols. London: Luzac, 1977.

____. *Studies in Islamic Mysticism.* Cambridge University Press, 1921.

Nurbakhsh, Javad. *Farhang-e Nurbakhsh,* 7 Vols. London, 1982-87.

____. *In The Tavern of Ruin.* New York, 1978.

____. *Jesus in the Eyes of the Sufis.* London, 1983.

____. *Spiritual Poverty in Sufism.* London, 1984.

____. *Sufism: Fear and Hope, Contraction and Expansion, Gathering and Dispersion, Intoxication and Sobriety, Annihilation and Subsistence.* New York, 1982.

____. *Traditions of the Prophet (Aḥâdith),* 2 Vols. New York,

Olfati Tabrizi, see Tabrizi.

Pickthall, Marmaduke, trans. *The Glorious Koran.* 1930 reprint. London: Allen & Unwin, 1969.

Qoshairi, Abo'l-Qâsem. *Tarjama-ye resâla-ye Qoshairi.* Edited by Badi'o'z-zamân Foruzânfar. Tehran, 1982.

Rumi, Jalâlo'd-Din. *Kolliyât-e Shams yâ Diwân-e kabir,* 10 Vols. Edited by Badi'o'z-Zamân Foruzânfar. Tehran, 1959.

——. *Mathnawi-ye ma'nawi.* Edited by R.A. Nicholson. Tehran, 1977.

Ruzbehân Baqli. *Mashrab al-arwâḥ.* Turkey, n.d.

——. *Sharḥ-e shaṭḥiyât.* Edited with notes, introduction, and indexes by Henry Corbin. Tehran, 1981.

Sabzawâri, Ḥâjji Mollâ Hâdi, (Asrâr). *Diwân-e Ḥâjji Mollâ Hâdi-ye Sabzawâri.* Edited by Sayyed Moḥammad Reḍhâ Dâ'i-Jawâd. Esfahan, n.d.

Sa'di. Moṣleḥo'd-Din. *Bustân.* Edited by Nuro'd-Din Irânparast. Tehran, 1977.

——. *Golestân.* Edited by Moḥammad 'Ali Forughi. Tehran, 1978.

Sanâ'i, Abo'l-Majd Majdud. *Diwân.* Edited by Modarres Raḍhawi. Tehran, 1975.

Sarrâj Ṭusi, Abu Naṣr. *Ketâb al-loma' fe't-taṣawwof.* E.J.W. Gibb Memorial Series, No.22. London, 1914.

Schimmel, Annemarie, *As Through a Veil: Mystical Poetry in Islam.* New York: Columbia Press, 1982.

——. *Mystical Dimensions of Islam.* Chapel Hill, 1975.

Shabestari, Maḥmud. *Golshan-e râz.* Edited by Javad Nurbakhsh. Tehran, 1976.

Shâh Dâ'i-ela'llâh Allâh Shirâzi, See Dâ'i Shirâzi.

Shâh Ne'mato'llâh Wali. *Kolliyât-e Shâh Ne'mato'llâh-e Wali.* Edited by Javad Nurbakhsh. Tehran, 1978.

——. *Rasâ'el-e Shâh Ne'mato'llâh-e Wali.* 4 Vols. Edited by Javad Nurbakhsh. Tehran, 1978.

Sohrawardi, Shehâbo'd-Din Abu Ḥafṣ 'Omar. *'Awâref al-ma'âref.* Bulaq, Egypt. 1872-3.

Solami, Abu 'Abdo'r-Raḥmân. *Ketâb ṭabaqât aṣ-ṣufiya.* Edited by Johannes Peterson. Leiden, 1960.

Steingass, F. *Persian-English Dictionary.* Tehran, 1976.

Ṭabasi, Darwish Moḥammad. *Âthâr-e Darwish Moḥammad Ṭabasi.* Edited by Iraj Afshâr and Moḥammad Taqi Dâneshpazhuh. Tehran, 1972.

Tabrizi, Sharafo'd-Din Ḥossain ebn Olfati. *Rashf al-alḥâz fi kashf al-alfâẓ.* Edited by Mâyel Herawi. Tehran, 1983.

Tahânawi, Moḥammad A'lâ ebn 'Ali. *Kashshâf eṣṭelâḥat al-fonun.* Edited by the Asiatic Society of Bengal. Calcutta, 1982.

Termedhi, Moḥammad ebn 'Ali. *Ketâb khatm al-auliyâ'.* Edited by

'Othmân Yaḥyâ. Beirut, 1965.
Vullers, Ioannis Augusti. *Lexicon Persico-Latinum.* 3 Vols. Reprint; 1855 Graz, 1962.
Wensinck, A.J., *Concordance et Indices de la Tradition Musulmane.* 6 Vols. Leiden: Brill, 1936.

INDEX OF PERSIAN AND ARABIC TERMS DEFINED IN THE TEXT

GENERAL INDEX

abad (post-eternity), III[1] 114, 66, 67.
Abraham, 19, 45, 46, 47, 72, 87, 142.
Abu Esḥâq ebn Shahriyar. See Kazerunie.
Abu Jahl (d. 624), 101
Abu 'Sa'id Abe'l-Khair (d.1049), 14, 25, 121, 153.
Adam, VI 73, 31, 57, 128, 163.
âghush (embrace), I 16, 53.
aḥadiyat (Oneness), 5, 17, 47, 56, 64, 155.
aḥadiyato'l-jam' (Oneness of Concentration), 51.
ahl-e wojud (finders), 77.
Ahmad ebn Ḥanbal (d. 855), 36.
'ain-e jam' (essence of concentration), 100.
'ain' o'l-yaqin (eye of certitude), 22.
'aish (delight), I 148, 90.
akhfâ (supraconscious), 15.
'âlam-e ghaib (world of the unseen), IV 120, 23, 26.
'âlam-e jabarut (world of power), IV 112, 75.
'âlam-e lahut, (relm of divinity), IV 116, 82.
'âlam-e malakut (angelic world), IV 108, 75.
'Ali ebn Tâleb (d. 661), 22, 162.
alif (familiar one), 90.
amr (command), 8.
anduh (anguish), 24, 40, *66*.
Anṣâri Herewi, Khwâja 'Abdo'l-lah (d. 1089), 4, 14, 113.
'aql-e ma'ad (other-worldly intellect), 25.
'aql-e ma'âsh (worldly intellect) 25.
'âref (gnostic), IV 89, 10, 21, 24, 31, 35, 36, 38, 57, 65, 68, 75, 77, 80, 81, 84, 91, 92, 93, 98, 101, 102, 105, 111, 112, 122, 132, 133, 142, 161, 162, 163, 169, 171, 172, 174, 176.
'asheq (lover), 15, 24, *48*.
'aṭâ' (bestowal), 17.
'Aṭṭâr Naishâburi, Farido'd-Din (d. 1220), 3, 9, 12, 28, 35, 39, 43, 44, 51, 55, 58, 61, 67, 76, 81, 82, 95, 97, 98, 99, 109, 125, 126, 127, 130, 136, 143, 145, 146.
awwaliyat (primacy), 67.
â'yân (essence), 105, 154.
â'yân-e thâbeta (permanent archetypes), 127.

1. Roman numerals and the numbers immediately following them denote the original Persian volume and page numbers where these terms have been defined infull.